NAZI ANTI-SEMITISM

NAZI ANTI-SEMITISM

From Prejudice to the Holocaust

PHILIPPE BURRIN

Translated by Janet Lloyd

THE NEW PRESS

NEW YORK
LONDON

Published in the United States by The New Press, New York, 2005
Distributed by W. W. Norton & Company, Inc., New York

The introduction and chapters 1–3 were originally published in
France as *Ressentiment et apocalypse: Essai sur l'antisémitisme nazi*
by Editions du Seuil, Paris, 2004.
Chapters 4–6 appeared in *Fascisme, nazisme, autoritarisme*
by Editions du Seuil, Paris, 2000.

LIBRARY OF CONGRESS CATALOGING-IN-PUBLICATION DATA

Burrin, Philippe, 1952–
Nazi anti-semitism : from prejudice to the Holocaust / Philippe Burrin.
p. cm.
"The introduction and chapters 1–3 were originally published in France as: Ressentiment
et apocalypse, 2004; chapters 4–6 appeared in Fascisme, nazisme, autoritarisme.
ISBN 1-56584-969-8 (hc.)
1. Antisemitism—Germany—History—20th century. 2. Fascism—Europe—
History—20th century. 3. National socialism—Europe—History—20th century.
4. Authoritarianism—Europe—History—20th century. 5. Holocaust, Jewish
(1939–1945)—Causes. I. Title.

DS146.G4B865   2005
940.53'18'0943—dc22   2005047900

The New Press was established in 1990 as a not-for-profit alternative to
the large, commercial publishing houses currently dominating the book publishing
industry. The New Press operates in the public interest rather
than for private gain, and is committed to publishing, in innovative ways, works of
educational, cultural, and community value that are often
deemed insufficiently profitable.

www.thenewpress.com

Composition by dix!

Printed in the United States of America

2   4   6   8   10   9   7   5   3   1

CONTENTS

INTRODUCTION

CAN GREAT TRAGEDIES have simple causes? They certainly give rise to simple questions, for it is as if the crushing magnitude of the event demands a single, all-encompassing explanation. Such questions are so daunting that historians understandably tend to shun grappling with them, preferring to study the question of "how" rather than "why." But is it really possible to avoid those questions, particularly in the case of the genocide of the Jews of Europe? That was a tragedy if ever there was one. It called our very civilization deeply into question, and it continues to stir the minds of many people, with views that range right across the spectrum.

On this subject, three questions insistently come to mind: Why was it that the tragedy took place in Germany, when aversion—at the very least, and, in many cases, hostility—to the Jews was widespread throughout Europe? Why did anti-Jewish prejudice become a kind of norm in German society after 1933, allowing the Nazi regime, whose anti-Semitism was far more radical than that of the general population, to implement its policies without encountering any serious obstacles? And why did the regime eventually settle on massacre when other solutions, ranging from a system of apartheid to enforced emigration or concentration in an outlying territory, were not only conceivable but were indeed adopted or at least considered?

One simple answer to these questions immediately presents itself: hatred of the Jews. But is that answer altogether satisfactory, and how can it be shown to be valid? The fact that anti-Semitism was part and parcel of the genocide goes without saying, and nobody bothers to challenge that. But the exact nature of that link—whether it was a direct relation of cause and effect or just a vague kind of solidarity—is a more controversial matter.

At first sight, the only explanation for the transgression of civilized boundaries, such as the massacre of defenseless people, including children, women, and old men, must surely be a hatred of exceptional intensity that stems from a deep reservoir of prejudice. To those who favor this line of reasoning, the genocide naturally appears as the paroxysmal outcome of the Christian world's long tradition of stigmatizing the Jews. From the nineteenth century onward, they claim, one particular national culture, that of Germany, developed an incomparably virulent strain of that anti-Semitism.

That is the argument presented by Daniel Goldhagen, whose thesis of a Germany with a "national plan" to "eliminate" the Jews chimes with a number of earlier works published at the end of World War II and even with the thesis of the existence of a "German mentality" that Emile Durkheim produced to explain the war crimes that the imperial armies committed on Belgian and French soil in the summer of 1914. Specialists have rightly criticized Goldhagen's selective interpretation and teleological reconstruction of pre-1933 German anti-Semitism. Similar criticism can justifiably be leveled against his notion of an unchanging anti-Semitism that remained a constant value from 1933 to 1945, for this fails to take into account the inculcation of prejudice among new generations that was used to fuel hostility to the Jews.

Such a trenchant thesis finds scant support in the scholarly community, in which many researchers tend, on the contrary, to qualify the importance that they ascribe to anti-Semitism. After all, does not a considerable hiatus set the cataclysmic character of the genocide apart from the banality or even "normality" of the anti-Semitism of the years both before and during the Nazi regime? Prejudice frequently bedevils and sometimes engulfs our societies without, however, leading to such tragedies, and it is no easy matter to show that hostility to the Jews had developed to an unprecedented degree in Europe or even in Germany in the years leading up to the catastrophe. Perhaps more account should be taken of other factors, either general and long-term or relevant to the immediate context of the Nazi regime.

The former category, that of general factors, includes the phenomenon of modernity, certainly a trend usually associated with positive connotations. The reason for drawing attention to it here, however, is not the emancipation and progress that it encourages, but the destructive potential that often constitutes its darker side, of which the Jewish genocide was a revealing manifestation. In the Nazi period and immediately after it, people following in the wake of Eric Voegelin were prone to pillory de-Christianization for having left the way open for the bloody idols, such as class and race, of totalitarian regimes. Nowadays, following in the steps of the philosopher Zygmunt Bauman, we prefer to blame the modern state, with its instrumental rationality and its cult of technology that led it to treat populations as objects to be recorded by a census—categorized, registered, and, sometimes, eliminated.

In support of this approach, one can point to the huge administrative apparatus upon which, from first to last, the Third Reich's policies of persecution depended. Its redoubtable efficiency certainly supports the thesis that Nazi racism was a highly modern technology and that the genocide of the Jews was a quite different operation from the genocide of the Tutsis of Rwanda in the 1990s. However, constitutional states, too, certainly resort to the use of the technological means of modernity just as the Nazi regime did, so it seems reasonable to wonder whether we are really on the track of the essential point here.

Many historians who specialize in the study of Nazi politics are (unlike those such as Saul Friedländer) prone to minimize the role played by anti-Semitism. Tracing the chain of decisions and the fabric of interactions that culminated in extermination, they tend to underline the role played by competing bureaucracies, the pressure of material or corporative interests, spiraling regional initiatives, and, in general, all the hesitations and improvisations that marked the process of persecution.

Their works have enriched our knowledge, but at some cost. Anti-Semitism, although always mentioned, is pushed into the background as a factor that should be taken into consideration and that is important above all because of the functions that it fulfilled, either by reanimating a Nazi party whose activism had stalled after its accession to power or by compensating the population for the regime's failure to deliver on its promises of social change. The genocide itself is portrayed as resulting from multiple constraints that, by rendering impossible other "solutions" to the "Jewish question," caused the choice to fall upon mass murder. In short, according to this view, the role played by anti-Semitism was simply that of drawing the persecutors' attention to a people traditionally stigmatized, whose elimination represented a kind of easy second-best, in default of achieving the entire racist recasting of Europe that the Nazi leaders had undertaken.

Clearly, both Christianity and modernity played a part in the genocide of the Jews, just as German history also, inevitably, did. But the extent to which they were involved and in what ways needs to be specified convincingly and on a comparative basis. We have been offered on the one hand an explanation that depends chiefly upon a long-term tendency favoring either Christian anti-Semitism or modernity, and on the other hand one that instead concentrates, sometimes in a quite shortsighted fashion, upon the meandering course of Nazi politics. It seems to me, however, that between the two there remains a whole neglected field of problems that needs to be addressed.

To establish the determining role that I believe anti-Semitism played in the Nazi policy of persecution, the best option is to choose a medium-term temporal framework— say from the end of the nineteenth century on—and to differentiate the object of our study. Modern anti-Semitism is usually treated as though it were all of a piece. At best, a distinction between its moderate and its radical forms is drawn, but with no indication of whether this is a matter of content or intensity. We need to recognize right from the start that anti-Semitism took many forms and that these included variants distinctive enough to ensure clear consequences in the determination of the measures that it would be desirable or acceptable to adopt. In the case of Germany, we must therefore first pinpoint the specificity of Nazi anti-Semitism and what there was about it that was relatively new, and then consider the extent to which it competed with or influenced the variants that existed alongside it.

The very internal diversity of anti-Semitism and the relative novelty of Nazi Judeophobia make it difficult to think purely in terms of continuity. The anti-Jewish tradition bequeathed by Christianity and absorbed by modern anti-Semitism patently carried considerable weight and there can be no question of minimizing it. But on the other hand we should not underestimate the importance of certain key events—in particular, the Nazis' accession to power in 1933—and, above all, the work of spreading and reshaping anti-Semitism that went ahead under the new regime.

It is not the case that after 1933 the Germans suddenly revealed themselves to be the anti-Semites that they had always been in secret. Rather, it was at this point that many more of them became anti-Semitic and more intensely so, as anti-Jewish prejudice became, so to speak, encrusted as a result of certain factors that need to be elucidated: some relate to the temporal medium-term, others to certain social mechanisms that accompanied the consolidation of the Nazi regime.

It seems clear that, viewed in such a perspective, anti-Semitism cannot be considered simply as a collection of negative clichés, let alone as a blind passion. It must also and above all be analyzed as a world of fantasies, a set of practices, and, more generally, as a culture—in other words, as a collection of representations that are used to define a collective identity and that must, consequently, be linked to other elements in that identity. An approach from the angle of cultural history must therefore endeavor to reconstruct the meaning that actors at the time ascribed to their anti-Jewish attitude or actions, and it must then relate that meaning to the wider political and national identity that surrounded it.

Such an approach has its limitations, as do probably most approaches to the subject of genocide. The historian stands on the brink of an abyss, attempting to probe its depths with extremely inadequate instruments. How can such hatred and violence be explained? The fact is that hatred must itself be fed by certain representations if it is to have any effect and be lasting. It relies upon certain themes and rationalizations, and it is these that we need to pinpoint while at the same time trying to understand the mechanisms by which German society appropriated them so thoroughly as to block all serious opposition to radical persecution.

Each of the chapters in Part I examines a particular aspect of the problem. The first tries to distinguish a possible specificity to the anti-Semitism of Germany and to this end adopts a comparative perspective within the medium-term temporal framework. Without claiming to resolve the matter, it raises the question of how to seize upon the anti-Semitic potential of a society or, put another way, upon the structural elements that may have afforded anti-Semitism greater chances to develop in Germany than elsewhere.

The second chapter focuses on Nazi anti-Semitism and its reception between 1933 and 1939. It attempts to define the sources of the radicalism of this anti-Semitism and to identify the mechanisms that enabled it to "speak" ever more powerfully to German society. In particular, it examines the link between hostility to the Jews and the identity of the majority population—a link that should make it possible to understand the dynamism that propelled anti-Semitic prejudice.

The third chapter is devoted to the mainsprings of the radicalization of Nazi policies during the war and to whatever made it possible to proceed from persecution based upon discrimination, spoliation, and forced emigration to extermination pure and simple. Such a radicalization was remarkable, given that the Jewish minority at that time found itself under the boot throughout Europe and also that the Nazi violence was not prompted by any threat from its victims. In other words, that radicalization stemmed from a fantastical interpretation of reality. We must try to decipher the inner reasoning behind that fantasy and understand what it was that rendered the German people so passive or so complicit.

In an overview of this type, it is hard to avoid being schematic or making insufficiently documented assertions.

Many years ago, Claude Lévi-Strauss drew attention to the dilemma posed by the choice between more explanation and less description, or vice versa. For me, what was important was to open up perspectives and formulate questions. It is up to my readers to decide upon the interest and pertinence of my suggested answers, and I hope to profit from their reactions.

* * *

Part II is a revised version of three lectures that I delivered at the Collège de France in Paris on April 23, May 4, and June 11, 2003, at the invitation of the Foundation in Memory of the Shoah. I would like to thank the directors, Mme. Simone Veil and M. Pierre Saragoussi, for doing me the honor of inviting me, and the Collège de France itself—in particular, its administrator, M. Jacques Glowinski—for its hospitality. Jean-Pierre Azéma and Henry Rousso were kind enough to chair these meetings. I thank them both and also Bronislaw Baczko for his comments on the manuscript.

These pages are part of a more wide-ranging work yet to be completed. My research has been greatly facilitated by the financial support provided by the Max Planck Prize that it was my honor to receive in 1997 and the fruitful periods that I spent at the Wissenschaftskolleg of Berlin (2000–2001) and at All Souls College, Oxford (Hilary term, 2003). This seems an excellent opportunity to express my gratitude to both institutions.

PART I

Resentment and Apocalypse

WHY GERMANY?

ANTI-SEMITISM WAS CLEARLY far from a phenomenon that was particularly, let alone exclusively, German. Throughout the region of Christian culture, to range no further afield, it had acquired the substance of a centuries-old tradition. Paradoxically, this was a tradition that modernity reformulated rather than weakened (as it did so many other phenomena) in radical fashion, at the same time delivering the technology that was to make the destruction of the Jews of Europe possible.

The genocide nevertheless came about in one particular place and at one particular time: in Germany, in the 1940s, after years of persecution. It is therefore justifiable to wonder whether there existed in that country factors that made the emergence and domination of an anti-Semitism capable of supporting a policy of genocide more probable than elsewhere. To attempt to answer that question, let us focus on a number of phenomena ranging from the general to the particular—namely, Christian anti-Judaism, modern anti-Semitism, and German anti-Semitism within the European framework.

What all these phenomena have in common is hostility to the Jews. As with xenophobia, this type of hostility is usually fueled by friction between the majority and a minority group. But such friction, whether religious, socioeconomic, or political, is as much imagined as real, perceived by the majority through the prism of prejudice. Furthermore, the strength and intensity of that prejudice likewise stem from the prevailing circumstances. Periods of economic crisis and political unrest particularly favor the adoption of anti-Semitic positions.

It is preferable, however, to underline a more general point—namely, the identifying function that anti-Jewish representations served for the majority social group. What precisely did anti-Semites do in this regard? On the basis of certain elements of reality, they constructed representations of a deforming and exaggerated nature that enabled them to erect frontiers between the Jews' identity and their own. Then, by underlining the differences and contrasts, or even constructing a thoroughly integral opposition, they emphasized their own values, and in this way, they shored up or, in some cases, redefined their own identity.

Anti-Semitism, like xenophobia and racism, is a weapon used in the struggle to assert an identity. It is a construction through which the majority society or, in most cases, just a fraction of that society expresses its anxieties and tensions and endeavors to overcome its doubts about its own identity. Hence the need to place at the center of our analysis the dialectic between negative images attributed to the Jews on the one hand and positive self-images on the other. That, in a nutshell, will be the guiding thread through this and the next two chapters.

*   *   *

Let us first adopt a long-term temporal perspective. History is certainly not short on conflicts between minority diasporas and the societies that receive them: the Armenians in the Ottoman Empire, the Chinese in Southeast Asia, and the Indians in East Africa all spring to mind. I think that what distinguishes the case of the Jews is the long-lasting, intense, and persistent nature of the antagonism manifested toward them. Judeophobia, to use a widely general term, is detectable in antiquity and has been continuously manifest ever since, even if the motivation behind it has varied, and likewise its intensity.

As is well known, that very persistence has fueled the arguments of anti-Semites, prompting them to blame the Jews themselves for the negative reactions from which they have suffered. Such arguments do not rate a long refutation since it is patently obvious that anti-Semitism is a problem created by anti-Semites. However, all prejudice is based upon perceptible differences which are then deformed and magnified, and the case of anti-Semitism is certainly no exception. It is fueled by three features that, when put together, produce a unique combination.

First, the Jewish people are identified by a religion, and that religion is indissociable from the Jews. This is not the case with other great religions, which are more universal and transcend the membership of any particular ethnic group.

Second, the Jewish religion was the root of the whole

monotheistic family of religions, and this has raised problems of rivalry for its "children," Christianity and Islam.
That rivalry has engendered a lasting hostility, particularly
between Christianity and Judaism, which are very closely related. On that account, it gives rise to particularly strong
tensions.

Christianity, which emerged from Judaism, established
with its predecessor a relationship that was characterized
both by the affiliation between the two, since Christianity
took over Judaism's hopes of a messiah, and also by the fact
that Christianity claimed to have surpassed Judaism, by realizing its hopes. This relationship profoundly altered the nature of the Judeophobia that had existed in the ancient
world and that had stemmed essentially from the clash between polytheism and monotheism. What had irritated the
pagan peoples of the ancient world had been the Jews' refusal to mingle with them and honor their gods. Christianity, for its part, elaborated an image of the Jews that linked
them far more closely to itself: the Jews were a people who
had passed on their tradition to Christianity but then, by ob-
stinately rejecting Christ's message, had aroused an intolera-
ble doubt as to the truth of the new religion. Although
shamed by that rejection and condemned to wander the
earth, the Jewish people nevertheless remained the witness
whose conversion at the Last Judgment would at last establish that truth forever.

The third feature distinguishing the Jewish people is the
fact that, ever since the destruction of the Temple, Jews have
constituted a diaspora, and, even after the creation of the
state of Israel, they have to a large extent remained one. The

lack of a territorial base—and consequently of any peasantry—created a socioeconomic asymmetry vis-à-vis the societies of Europe, which, for their part, accentuated this by imposing upon the Jews professional constraints that fueled lasting tensions, particularly given the Jews' specialization in professions involving the management of money.

Down through the centuries, Judeophobia has been spurred by variable combinations of religious intolerance, xenophobia, and socioeconomic friction. At one time or another, each of these has been exploited by the Church, elite social groups, and the masses, all bent upon serving their own interests or passions. But it was Christianity, as the major cultural framework, that provided the vocabulary, themes, and rhetoric required to voice hostility to the Jews. All the same, it would be an exaggeration to postulate a constant hostility. As tends to happen between closely related sects or religions, relations were certainly strained during the first millenium, particularly in the late Roman Empire, once Christianity became the state religion. But they were never marked by a particularly high level of violence.

It was not until the twelfth century that in northern Europe (England, Germany, and France), a region until then peripheral but at this point expanding fast, a form of Judeophobia developed that was considerably more violent because of a new dimension of imagined behaviors, including accusations that Jews engaged in ritual murder, profanation of the host, and the poisoning of wells. Historians have suggested a variety of reasons to explain this development. Some have to do with theological shifts, and in particular the emphasis now laid on the representation of a suffering

Christ, which made the Jewish people—as the deicide—seem more repulsive than ever. Other reasons are connected to socioeconomic tensions, and in particular the commercialization of the economy, which created a privileged position for some Jews, giving them a high profile in the world of trade and taxation.

At any rate, it was at this point that what the historian Kevin Langmuir has called the chimerical (that is to say, fantastical) dimension to Judeophobia made its appearance. It was a dimension that distinguished Judeophobia from the hostility displayed to other minorities. The Jews were now accused of essentially evil behavior that took absurd forms such as the killing of Christian children in order to use their blood in religious rituals. This then gave rise to imaginary representations of a daunting perversity, for they firmly associated the idea of a wildly disproportionate malignancy with the situation of the tiny minority of Jews, thereby compounding the scorn that the dominant social group professed for the Jews with an element of irrational fear. In extraordinary circumstances such as those of the Crusades or epidemics, this could easily unleash the very worst excesses of violence. The idea of Jewish malignancy then became so rooted in tradition that this fantastical representation continued to fuel itself, even when no Jews were present.

The long history of the discrimination and expulsions that plagued the Jews in medieval Europe (far more than they ever did in Islamic countries in this period) is closely linked with this combination of particular circumstances. All the same, it should be remembered that the protection that the ecclesiastical authorities afforded the Jews, though limited, did operate as a real brake. If the Church had treated the Jews as a whole as it treated heretics, it is doubtful whether any at all would have survived in Europe.

In the seventeenth century, and above all the eighteenth, the situation changed thanks to the Enlightenment, which questioned the authority of the Church and, in the name of reason, attacked all prejudice. Inasmuch as it defended equal rights and a religious neutralization of public space, the current of liberalism played a role of capital importance in the emancipation of the Jews, which spread gradually from West to East, affecting France in 1790–1791, the countries of central Europe around 1870, and reaching Russia in 1917. It offered the Jews the best conceivable position even if, when associated with nationalism, it sometimes cultivated a desire for assimilation that was hard to distinguish from an eradication of Judaism pure and simple.

The Enlightenment also had its less luminous aspects. In some sectors (consider the example of Voltaire), Judeophobia found new vigor. Paradoxically enough, de-Christianization gave Judeophobia a new lease on life. It increased the irritation aroused by Jewish particularism and increased distaste for Jewish monotheism, now held to be the source of all fanaticism and obscurantism. This attitude was to persist in the following century's current of atheism and materialism.

It would be unfair, however, to portray such developments as the major contribution of the Enlightenment. After all, the emancipation of the Jews that it engendered was a matter of justice. All the same, the movement was instrumental in disrupting Jewish life, since it dissolved the traditional community and presented to individuals a wide range of choices that had never been theirs before, whether they leaned toward traditionalism, liberalism, socialism, or zionism.

These upheavals affected anti-Semites very little. In fact, their hostility strengthened just at the time when the Jewish world was becoming increasingly diversified. Some historians use the expression "modern anti-Semitism" to describe this time. Others, to be sure, reject that description, and it is certainly not hard to show the extent to which the new discourse in fact substantially perpetuated the Christian tradition of stigmatizing the Jews. However, it is important also to underline the relative novelty of this discourse, for in at least three respects it expressed a change of paradigm.

In the first place, the context in which anti-Semitic discourse now appeared, which was to remain its context of reference thereafter, was new. It was characterized by the approximate coincidence between the emancipation of the Jews and the modernization of European societies. Equal rights were granted to the Jews just as Europe, or at least western and central Europe, was being revolutionized by industrialization, urbanization, the politicization of the masses, and nationalism.

Now, for multiple reasons—in particular, their long-standing urbanization, their socioprofessional specialization, their tradition of literacy, and their connections among the diaspora—the Jews were among the first to benefit from the advantages of modernization. Their relative success (which, however, should not mask the general poverty of the Jewish masses in eastern Europe) gave rise to the idea that they were, if not the instigators, at least the main beneficiaries of the changes that were taking place. This provoked irritation and hostility on the part of not only the social strata adversely affected by modernization, but also those who were upwardly mobile—in particular, the university-educated bourgeoisie, which now found itself in competition with the Jews. The Jews were thus identified first with liberalism, then with socialism and communism—in short, with everything that was undermining the hold of tradition and boding ill for stability.

Hostility simultaneously stemmed from another development: the recomposition of identities around the concept of nationality. This cast the diasporic situation of the Jews into even greater relief and encouraged other groups to challenge their assimilation in the name of homogeneity or national cohesion.

Modern anti-Semitism thus developed in reaction to emancipation and what appeared to be its dire consequences—namely, the material success and presumed power of the Jews. Among the works in which this reaction first found expression was one published in 1845 by the French Alphonse Toussenel, entitled *Les Juifs, rois de l'époque* (The Jews, the Kings of the Age). Virtually the same title, in a variety of forms, was then used for works that appeared in most other European languages, all of them drawing attention to what was seen as a scandalous situation: the despised minority was fast becoming a power that threatened to bend the Christian world to its will and might even take revenge against its erstwhile persecutors.

Representations of the ubiquity, cohesion, and otherness of the Jews, together with the image of a secretly plotting power and the new world conditions—with all the confusion and destabilization that such rapid change engenders, particularly with regard to the traditional frontiers between religious confessions, social strata, the genders, and so on—all combined to fuel the anti-Jewish fantasy.

A second paradigm change, directly stemming from the foregoing, had modern anti-Semitism drawing upon a wider range of themes. It could be linked to three forms of collective identity that were formally competing with each other but that were frequently intertwined in practice: religion, nation, and race. Thus three different variants of anti-Semitism can typically, or in theory, be distinguished.

Christian anti-Semitism prolonged traditional anti-Judaism and, right down to the early twentieth century, sporadically revived the accusation of ritual murder. But at the same time, it enriched that anti-Judaism with new themes drawn from the situation of religion challenged by the process of secularization and striving to react or take action against this by making use of associations, political parties, and the press. Anti-Semitism became a subsidiary aspect to an identity endeavoring to adapt to the challenge that the modern age posed to the traditional bases of Christian society.

Soon, however, as the nation became the framework of allegiance for most Europeans, it was national anti-Semitism that came to predominate. The Jews were believed to constitute a political, economic, or cultural threat to this national framework by reason of their lust for power or their transnational solidarity. It is worth noting that this variant of anti-Semitism—which, from the end of the nineteenth century on, was to reinforce resistance to Jewish immigration from eastern Europe—did make allowances for an equivalent to conversion within the framework of Christian anti-Semitism. It accepted Jews into the nation—preferably in limited numbers—provided they had proved the reality of their assimilation by a long period of residence and participation in the defense of the homeland. The exemptions that Hitler was forced to concede in 1933 for Jewish veterans who had fought for Germany—exemptions which, however, were to prove no more than temporary—testify to the force of this variant of anti-Semitism. Other examples could be found within the French political Right after 1918 (the case of Barrès is well known, and Maurras followed the same line of reasoning).

In the third shift in rhetoric, racist anti-Semitism developed in the late nineteenth century by appropriating notions that were at this time surrounded by a scientific aura, even though their validity was increasingly being questioned. Racism, after all, aimed to account for human diversity using the methods of the natural sciences. The new late-nineteenth-century wave of European overseas imperialism and the diffusion of social Darwinism won it popularity. Racism lent scholarly prestige to ancient prejudices just as had the distinction between Semites and Indo-Europeans borrowed from linguistics. At any rate, once applied to the Jews, it created an uncrossable frontier. The determinism of "blood" ruled out both conversion and assimilation. Although this current of anti-Semitism remained very limited, that did not prevent its rhetoric from spreading widely.

These three variants of anti-Semitism shared common

themes. They were all characterized by syncretism, or the capacity to amalgamate around their organizing principle the greater part of the baggage of anti-Jewish images and stereotypes bequeathed by the Christian tradition, bringing these up-to-date (for example, the "Mammonism" of the Jews) and adding new images: the Jew as a corrupter of national culture, the revolutionary Jew, the Jew fomenting a "Jewish war" in order to amass profits and force nations that resisted the Jews to massacre one another, and so on. Furthermore, all three variants resorted to the same tropes of decadence and plotting. To the extent that it was mainly expressed by the sectors of society that were suffering most from modernization and resented this as an aggression against their own identity, modern anti-Semitism acquired a murky tinge, permanently veined by images of violence. This happened despite the fact that the measures recommended by the anti-Semites were not necessarily all of a violent nature, ranging as they did from a partial or total abrogation of emancipation all the way to expulsion or massacre.

At any rate, modern anti-Semitism formed a corpus of clichés that was to remain essentially unchanged right up to the present day. It circulated widely, even crossing frontiers, thanks to new means of communication, and became an aggressive weapon in the field of mass politics that was emerging at the end of the nineteenth century. Modern anti-Semitism was a means of populist mobilization, particularly against liberal regimes. Parties that made anti-Semitism the central, or even sole, point of their programs were making an appearance as early as the 1880s, although admittedly they did not win more than marginal support. But anti-Semitism had by then become a theme that could be integrated into quite a wide variety of political platforms.

The last paradigm change relates to the place held by the Jews in the modern anti-Semitic identity, a place far more central than it held in Christianity. For modern anti-Semitism, particularly in its national and, above all, its racist variants, constructed an image of the Jews as the absolute opposite and total negative of the identity that it was itself defending and championing. Their physical, moral, and cultural characteristics were represented by a dualist system that placed them, term for term, in opposition to the characteristics of the anti-Semites: nomads versus those with a fixed seat of habitation, gold versus blood, lies versus truth, cowardice versus heroism. Even religion was not spared. Religion was declared too noble for the Jews and was denied them. Judaism was considered at the very most a code of behavior designed to regulate the lives of the Jews among themselves and the relations between Jews and Gentiles (whom they were, it was said, remorselessly encouraged to cheat).

It is important to stress that the more the Jews served as a negative reference in any definition of identity, the more dangerous the anti-Semitism that resulted, for the Jews then symbolized everything that the anti-Semites needed to eliminate in order to allow their own identity to flourish. (In this sense, contrary to Goldhagen's thesis, there was nothing specifically German about "elimination." It lay at the very heart of radical modern anti-Semitism.) The mechanism functioned all the more rigorously whenever what was at stake was a new identity—not an already rooted one such as a national identity, but the newly invented identity of the Aryan, the Germanic, or Nordic man. In short, the opposite figure of the Jew occupied a place that was all the more important because the "positive" figure itself possessed fewer concrete characteristics and less historical reality.

When it comes to defining radical anti-Semitism, this aspect seems more pertinent than the presence of any racist grid. Any anti-Semitism that—whether for religious, national, or racist motives, or, more likely, for a combination of all three—placed the Jews at the center of the definition of the anti-Semite's identity, as the negative opposite of that identity, was bound to be of a radical nature, for it implied that the fulfilment of the anti-Semite identity depended upon the disappearance of the Jewish identity right here and now.

Until 1914 this type of radical construction was seized upon only by small minorities. Far more widespread was the kind of anti-Semitism that constituted a "cultural code" (to borrow the expression favored by the historian Shulamit Volkov)—that is to say, the crystallization of a whole series of prejudices aroused by the modern world—or that was simply a private aversion, both of which themselves stemmed from the clash between all the scorned characteristics of the Jews on the one hand and all that non-Jews defined as their own identity on the other.

*　*　*

What was the situation around 1900? Anti-Semitism, at least in the form of a latent prejudice, was rife throughout Europe and also in the United States. However, in public life, its presence in political debate, or as an instigator of discriminatory legislation, was uneven. This lack of uniformity was due to a variety of factors, one being the size of the Jewish population—although, as the Hungarian part of the Hapsburg Empire shows, this was not necessarily a determining factor. It was less important than the degree of modernization and the type of political culture.

By and large, the situation was the most favorable to the Jews in countries with liberal regimes and a commercial culture, such as England and Holland, and it was the least favorable in authoritarian states with a religious basis and an agrarian/monarchical culture, such as Romania and Russia. These were countries prone to pogroms and where emancipation remained blocked. Between those two extremes, the situations of France and Germany were quite similar, while Austria-Hungary represented a kind of transition between western and eastern Europe.

In contrast to the situation in England and Holland, vociferous groups of anti-Semites on both sides of the Rhine made their presence felt, and the so-called "Jewish question" was widely and hotly debated. The debate was spurred on by the Jews' "success" in commerce and finance and even more by their "visibility," perceived through a prism marked by prejudice, in sectors where they were newcomers, such as education, the liberal professions, and public administration, not to mention the corridors of political power in the France of the Third Republic.

To be sure, anti-Semitism was at the same time contained by important counterweights, at the level of both the political parties and the legal system, where emancipation was guaranteed by a constitutional state. Such counterweights were probably more effective in France since, for one thing, the mind-set of elite groups there, particularly in the universities, was less hostile than in Germany.

Nevertheless, in both these countries anti-Semitism possessed the potential to abrogate emancipation at least partially. Indeed, following a series of asynchronous developments, it succeeded in doing so (in Germany in 1933 and in France in 1940). At the turn of the twentieth century, it was France, in the wake of its Dreyfus affair, that presented an unedifying spectacle of anti-Jewish demonstrations. After 1918, on the contrary, it was in Germany that anti-Semitism became strident, a tendency that intensified from 1930 onward. The situation had more or less calmed down in France in the 1920s, but in the following decade anti-Semitism flared up again quite strongly, even in radical forms that found striking expression in the works of writers such as Céline. In hindsight, the relative calm of the twenties seems more circumstantial than fundamental.

What is certain, however, is that in both France and Germany the disappearance of democratic regimes cleared the way for a discriminatory anti-Semitism that triumphed as a result of quite similar causes in the two countries: the combination of an internal crisis, an external war, and a defeat. In Germany, the sequence was war, defeat, crisis; in France, crisis, war, defeat. In both countries, a national crisis triggered a search for scapegoats and a move to seek reassurance in an identity defined in ethnic terms. It is true that in the case of France, the Jewish Statute was adopted by the Vichy regime at a time when the country was partly occupied by Nazi Germany. But there can be no doubt about the spontaneous and voluntary nature of this anti-Semitic legislation. In Germany, judging from the way that the conservative parties there developed from 1930 on, an abrogation of emancipation would already have been in the cards, given an authoritarian restructuring of the political regime, even without Adolf Hitler's accession to power.

The fact remains, however, that in Germany the change did not stop at an abrogation of emancipation but eventually led to genocide. Admittedly, the change was brought about by a regime whose key party had already acquired an important place in the moribund Weimar Republic. Even if the Nazis never obtained a majority of votes (President Hindenberg included the Nazis in a coalition government in which they initially held a minority position), they had rallied a degree of support that no party of the extreme right in France ever obtained, even at the height of the 1930s crisis. In Germany, anti-Semitism constituted a major element in the Nazi agenda, and while this probably motivated no more than a fraction of the electors, it clearly did not deter the rest from voting for Nazi representatives.

Given that the situation in France was relatively close to that in Germany, what can be the explanation for this disparity in excess? In an attempt to discover the answer, we can adopt the notion of limited causality proposed by Raymond Aron, and ask ourselves what the conditions would have to be without which a radical form of anti-Semitism such as the Nazi variant would probably never have emerged and flourished. To that end, we need to reflect upon all that was likely

to strengthen the perception of a Jewish "difference" regarded as malignant. This involves addressing the identifying problems that beset German society and incited it to
regard the Jews as the partial or total cause of those problems.

Even before 1914 there existed three structural elements
that, with circumstances abetting, were likely to fuel any
anti-Semitic potential. Of those three elements, only one,
the last, was not specific to Germany.

The first element was of a national nature and stemmed
from the famous "German question." This had come to the
fore at the time of the 1848 revolution, when two possible
concepts of Germany came into confrontation: "Little Germany" and "Greater Germany." The second concept implied bringing together all the Germans of central Europe in
a single state, but it was the first concept that Bismarck
adopted in 1871, leaving the Germans in Austria beyond the
frontiers of Germany.

However, this was no more than a provisional solution,
for the new state, with its identity centered on the Prus-
sian Hohenzollern dynasty, was obviously not as solidly
grounded as such ancient formations as England or France.
In short, the new state needed to forge a common identity
that could be shared by citizens set apart from one another
by all kinds of particularities. When a national-liberal such as
Heinrich von Treitschke justified his anti-Semitism by referring to the fragility of the new state, he was voicing an anx-
ious concern that was by no means feigned and certainly not
isolated. This anxiety rendered the presence of the Jews,
with their own specific identity and their sudden "success"

all the more irritating, for by contrast it seemed to accentuate the German difficulty.

The young age of the German state no doubt strengthened the aspiration to create a homogeneously ethnic community, and that tendency was also encouraged by other
factors: (1) the fact that Germany was a country that produced many emigrants, which favored a definition of nationality founded upon blood rights to avoid a loss of contact
with its German expatriates; (2) the colonial experience,
which gave rise to a veritable obsession with "crossbreeding" between German colonists and African populations;
and (3) the struggle against existing minorities within the
Reich—in particular, against the Polish minority in the east,
whose religious difference and cultural particularism constituted a strong irritant. The tendency was further supported
by a nationalistic current that the romanticism of the early
nineteenth century infused with hostility to the "Western"
world of liberalism and capitalism and that found emphatic
expression toward the end of the century in the *völkisch* wave
of ethnoracist-based nationalism.

In truth, the tendency to value an ethnic identity above all
else compounded the problem, for it drew attention to the
fact that many Germans still remained beyond the frontiers
of the new state. In fact, hardly had a dynastic/state identity
been consolidated than it was challenged by a pan-
Germanist movement. The latter now made its appearance
both within the Reich and in the German part of the Hapsburg empire. The effects of its challenge were even felt further afield since a number of forms of identity, such as a
Germano-Nordic variant that ignored national frontiers in

the common sense of the term now emerged simultaneously. As the future Reich's partisans saw it, its duty was to unite not only populations with a Germanic culture but also peoples of Germano-Nordic descent (such as Scandinavians, the Dutch, and the Flemish).

Imperialism was an integral part of the political aspirations of all these currents. It found expression in the idea of a continental empire to be conquered at the expense of Russia, an empire that could be appropriated by means of colonization simply by forcibly displacing some of its Slavic inhabitants. The risk of instability raised by the new German state by reason of its growing power and its situation in the middle of Europe was now considerably increased. Inevitably, this worried the Jews, for not only were trends such as *völkisch* nationalism in general fundamentally hostile to them, but German designs in eastern Europe, where the majority of European Jews were living, did not bode well.

Even if those tendencies remained limited until 1914, they were emblematic of a wider problem of identity that harbored an undeniable anti-Semitic potential. Anything that could underline the "German question" was likely to reinforce an ethnic definition of nationhood, and this was bound to aggravate the perception of Jewish "otherness," and at the same time that of other categories, such as Gypsies.

The second element that fueled anti-Semitic potential was of a religious nature and stemmed from the influence that religion wielded in German society and the irritation caused by the confessional division. The weight carried by the religious factor resulted from the fact that secularization in Germany was less marked than it was in France where, in the early twentieth century, the secular republic had clashed with the world of Catholicism. In Germany, in contrast, the imperial regime was based on an alliance between throne and altar, as was reflected in institutional practices such as the noting of religious affiliation in official documents and the state's levying of an ecclesiastical tax.

It is worth adding that, right from the start, German nationalism had been infused by Christian religiosity. The Protestants, who made up two-thirds of the population of the new state, had identified, body and soul, with the 1871 empire, regarding it as the culmination of the Reformation. Even in the Catholic world, despite the sharp sense of bitterness left by the *Kulturkampf,* people progressively rallied to imperial nationalism. During World War I, Protestants and Catholics alike adopted a rhetoric that presented the war as a divine trial for a Germany entrusted with a particular mission that set it apart, on the famous *Sonderweg,* from the liberal and commercial West.

At any rate, it was widely believed that the nation needed a religious bond. The confessional division between Protestants and Catholics constituted an obstacle to this, at least in the eyes of those who wished for a closer link and regarded that division as a serious weakness or even as the cause of German impotence ever since the religious wars. When the *völkisch* thinker Paul de Lagarde spoke of the need for a "national religion," he was expressing an idea that exercised many people's minds.

Just as pan-Germanism sharply reflected this latent irritation with the problem of nationality, so the *völkisch* movement did where religion was concerned. In fact, the *völkisch* movement aspired to be a movement of reform at once political and religious. Nothing similar existed in France, where the nationalistic current drew support from Catholicism and exalted it in the name of the "true France" in the battle against Republicanism, which was considered to be a source of decadence. Nobody in France dreamed either of reforming the Catholic religion or of proposing a substitute religion (actually, a substitute religion already existed, but on the left, in the guise of Freemasonry).

In Germany, in contrast, the idea of reform at once political and religious had taken root, as is testified by two peculiar movements that originated in *völkisch* circles. The first was that of the "German Christians," who wished to purge Christianity of its Judaic origins and restore it, in its original "purity," to those for whom it had always been destined—namely, the German people. The second, smaller movement was that of the "German believers," who denounced the idea of purging Christianity as illusory and desired instead to break with Christianity and return to the ancient religion of the Germans, a pantheism that did not recognize any ideas of original sin or love for one's neighbor.

Both movements testify to the strength of the aspiration to endow the Germans with a single common religion of an ethnic or ethnoracist nature. Both were fundamentally anti-Semitic, as was logical enough, given that Judaism was regarded as the force that had corrupted the original anti-Semitic Christianity or, worse still, as having invented an entirely Jewish Christianity. All this was a far cry from the traditional Christian anti-Judaism.

The last structural element affecting anti-Semitic potential was of a political nature, and was the clout that the authoritarian culture carried in German society. Some historians have called into question the theory of Germany's *Sonderweg* or "particular development," pointing out that Germany differed from the countries of western Europe only in degree, not by nature. However, one is bound to recognize that in Germany, the aristocratic groups still carried considerable weight and that the bourgeoisie there, without being "feudalized," did treat them with remarkable deference. Besides, more generally, liberalism, usually the guarantor of emancipation for the Jews, rapidly became wedded to nationalism and proved too weak to imbue the political culture with its own fundamental values, starting with individualism.

In Germany, the authoritarian culture was not limited to the strictly political field. It was also manifest in the tendency to ascribe to social values such as order, punctuality, cleanliness, and industriousness the importance that is attached elsewhere to universal political values such as those proclaimed by the American and French revolutions. Those "secondary values," as we should call them nowadays, were represented as being typically German. They reinforced an ethnic concept of the German identity while being functional with regard to the needs of a modern society.

The authoritarian culture was also evident in a strong tendency to set a high value on power. This manifested itself in the cult of the army and military values and also in intolerance of political divisions that might obstruct the young state's conquest of "a place in the sun." Seeking to explain the Nazi phenomenon, Norbert Elias stresses the importance of the memory of Germany's international weakness in preceding centuries. The cultivated memory of that past lack of power, which was quite the opposite of the optimistic foreign policy culture of another country also then on the rise—the United States—was to encourage Germany's tense aspirations for power.

In short, each of the elements mentioned here—ethnic nationalism, religious reinvigoration, and authoritarian national values—was potentially liable to accentuate perception of the "otherness," or, rather, the "malignity," of the Jews. Prior to 1914, that potential was contained by barriers that the postwar years initially reinforced, thanks to the installation of the Weimar Republic. However, as is well known, the republic never had time to become rooted, and the potentialities for anti-Semitism were, for their part, already being activated by a multiplicity of crises connected with national identity.

After the end of World War I, the "German question" became more acute than ever. The destruction of the traditional European empires left compact pockets of Germans in the new states that appeared all around the Reich—in Austria (it should be remembered that the Treaty of Versailles specifically forbade the reunion of the two countries), in the Sudetan region, and in Poland—and at the same time, many of the strategic deterrents with the power to block any new expansion on the part of Germany disappeared. Combined with the shock of defeat, this situation lent strong encouragement to the diffusion of ethnic nationalism.

The churches, for their part, found themselves challenged

by the way that German society was evolving. Protestantism was particularly affected since, with the disappearance of the empire, it lost its role as the pillar of the throne, and this was to make it a likely source of Nazi voters. The Catholics, in contrast, benefited from the establishment of the new regime and, along with the Social Democrats, now became one of its principal sources of support. However, in the face of the growing secularization of the public domain, the liberalization of mores, and, of course, the risk of a revolution, they shared the deep anxiety of the Protestants. This movement of reaction and the shared desire for a re-Christianization of society explains the welcome offered to the Nazi regime in 1933, even in Catholic circles, which then progressively abandoned their initial reservations.

Finally, at the political level, the Weimar Republic suffered right from the start from the conditions in which it was set up and from a series of subsequent shock waves. The nationalists delighted in stigmatizing their opponents for their links with foreigners: they identified liberalism with the yoke imposed by the victors, communism with Bolshevik Russia and Catholicism with Ultramontanism. Simultaneously, wartime shortages and postwar crises were causing people to fall back in desperation upon the "secondary values" while the growing attraction of a cult of the body and sanitary purging, directed in particular against venereal diseases, encouraged a broader spread of eugenics than elsewhere.

All the evidence seems to point to a Germany in thrall to a crisis of identity. A deep-seated resentment developed as a result of the disappearance of the imperial regime and nostalgia for the prewar period now, with hindsight, perceived as a golden age; the loss of the status of a great power, accompanied by an ever more pressing "German question"; the deep undermining of social strata in which self-esteem suffered from economic crises caused first by the hyperinflation of the early 1920s, then by the 1929 depression; and finally, all the frustrations felt by German Christians. From 1930 on, this, in its turn, made many Germans receptive to the appeal of Nazism's mixture of plebiscitarian Caesarism, an ethnoracist chauvinism that ignored existing frontiers, a pseudo-Christian religiosity, and a quest for power. In a society in which many citizens yearned to set a new high value upon a Christian and authoritarian German identity, tolerance for the otherness of the Jews was bound gradually to shrink, just like Balzac's proverbial *peau de chagrin*.

2

JUDEOPHOBIA AND
THE NAZI IDENTITY

NAZISM'S ACCESSION TO power in 1933 certainly marked a turning point of the greatest importance. However, there was still a long way to go before Auschwitz, and we now need to examine the problem of how that destination was reached.

The problem can be divided into two questions. The first concerns the dynamics of the persecution that was unleashed as early as 1933 and from then on never ceased to gather momentum. What was the mainspring of that dynamism? Many historians consider it to have been the very way in which the Nazi regime functioned—its polycratic structure and the intrinsic irrationality that allowed it to achieve only negative objectives such as the persecution inflicted upon the Jews. Although this thesis of a "cumulative radicalization," as Hans Mommsen puts it, may contain an element of truth, it discounts the propulsive force of ideology too easily by ascribing to the latter an inconsistency and incoherence that disqualify it as a grid by which to read the world and as a table of orientation for action. We must first check whether it did not, on the contrary, possess considerable coherence and whether a fundamental radicalism was not an inherent part of this.

The second question is one that does not always receive as much attention: What of the German population? The new regime tried hard to imbue it with its own anti-Semitism, and, given that it undoubtedly succeeded, we must identify the means that made this possible. This is an important point, for the absence of any substantial opposition also contributed to the dynamism of the persecution.

*   *   *

It is frequently said of Hitlerian ideology that it contained nothing new and was a potpourri of notions already present in modern anti-Semitism more or less everywhere. This is quite true if one looks no further than the catalogue of its representations and themes: the Jew as an exploiter and a parasite, the Jew as a manipulator and a revolutionary, the Jew as a poisoner and a carrier of infection. All those images had been circulating throughout the continent for several decades, but if we wish to see beyond that inventory, we must seek what it was that fundamentally structured Hitlerian anti-Semitism and, to that end, pay serious attention to the picture that emerges from an attentive reading of *Mein Kampf.*

What do we find there? Above all, a racist ideology—an ideology that considers race to be the explanatory principle of the history of the world. Hitler, a racist thoroughly in agreement with that ideology, postulates the existence of human races as separate from one another as the animal species and arranged in a hierarchy according to how they are evaluated. Positioned at the top of the hierarchy is the Aryan race, the sole creator of culture, as is "proved" by the great empires of antiquity, particularly those of Greece and Rome. Beneath, midway down the hierarchy, are races such as the Japanese, which preserve the fund of culture by assimilating that of the Aryans, particularly their technology, into their own lives. At the bottom of the hierarchy, according to this ideology, are the Jews, who create nothing, have no state or culture of their own, and are parasites living at the expense of the other peoples of the earth, which they inexorably destroy.

According to Hitler, the evolution of the human races established the decisive importance of two "laws of nature" that applied to the entire living world. One was the law of racial purity, racial endogamy, whose violation through interbreeding leads to decadence and eventual extinction. The other was the law of selection, or the elimination of the weak in combat or through a deliberate eugenic policy.

Such an ideology is strictly racist, for it focuses not only upon "aliens"—all those who are defined, by whatever criteria, as not belonging to the superior race—but also upon the members of that superior race itself, only some of whom (the best) must be encouraged to procreate while the rest, "the tainted," must be excluded from reproduction and even from "the banquet of life" itself. Unsurprisingly, Hitler emphatically praised the breeding system for horses and dogs and espoused the social Darwinist idea of a struggle for survival. His morality was of an ancient or, to be more precise, Germanic nature. His constant praise of "toughness" conveyed a desire to destroy the moral barriers of existing civilization, with all its humanitarianism and universalism, and to link up once more with a pre-Christian civilization ruled by ethnic exclusivism and the law of the strongest, which justified the extermination or enslavement of all conquered peoples.

All of this is cast in a biologizing register that testifies to the strength of Hitler's "scientism." But Hitler did not confine himself within this framework, for he also related the so-called "laws of nature" to "the Eternal One," or to "the Lord." He invoked not the personal god of monotheism but a deity confused with Creation, who remains forever mysterious, in contrast to the "laws of nature," which human reason can decipher and which, he recommended, should be observed.

Hitler established a link not only between the "laws of nature" and some kind of transcendence, but also with history, since historical understanding is the means for verifying the validity of all these so-called "laws." He did this when sketching in a history of the Aryans that followed a precise schema. The Aryan peoples, whose supposed superiority stemmed from their being endowed with idealism (a spirit of devotion to the community, reflected in the way they worked and fought), and who respected blood purity and practiced selection: for example, they killed deformed children at birth. In this way, they acquired such power that they were able to conquer peoples far greater numerically and to use them as slaves in the construction of great empires. These empires gave rise to brilliant cultures but then declined, allegedly owing to their eventual interbreeding with the peoples they had conquered.

This historical schema was also a model. Nazism's mission was to restore Germany to a rank of power by curing it of the decadence that afflicted it, thereby enabling it to conquer an empire comparable to those of the past in every respect, including cultural greatness. At the heart of Nazism lay this imperial mission. Through every page of *Mein Kampf* can be glimpsed a portrait of Hitler *imperator.*

An anti-Semitic ideology nestles at the heart of this racist framework. The history of the races' battle for survival is immemorial, but for two millennia a struggle had been raging between two races in particular, whose respective characteristics rendered them perfectly antagonistic. The characteristics of the Jews placed them, term for term, as ignoble is opposed to noble, in opposition to the Aryans. They supposedly possessed no idealism and consequently no solidarity, except in situations of danger or in order to lay hold of some prey. They had no religion—only a simple code of practical behavior—no culture other than through imitation, and no state, since they were incapable of organizing one. All they did have, in abundance, was deception, the weapon par excellence that enabled them to live as parasites leeching on other people by getting them to believe that they, the Jews, were assimilable into their nations. On the other hand, they did observe the so-called "laws of nature" and so preserved the purity of their blood. This made them redoubtable in their pursuit of power, as was allegedly illustrated by their project of world domination, which Hitler claimed to be attested by the *Protocols of the Elders of Zion,* a Tsarist forgery that continues, even today, to be circulated by anti-Semites.

This historically determining struggle between Aryans and Jews began when primitive Christianity—proclaimed, of course, by an Aryan and therefore anti-Semitic Christ—was distorted by the Jew Paul, who turned it into a form of universalism that, just like the Bolshevism that it spawned much later, was to encourage the spread of crossbreeding and decadence, thereby greatly profiting the Jews. Ever since, that struggle had become increasingly intense, particularly in the nineteenth century and during World War I. At the time Hitler was writing *Mein Kampf,* he claimed that it was still ongoing, taking two forms that were contradictory only in appearance: one the class warfare propagated by Bolshevism (a supposed Jewish invention), the other the internationalization of economies, brought about by the Jewish financiers of the Anglo-Saxon countries. According to Hitler, the outcome of the struggle, through which the Jews aimed to destroy not only the nations of the world but the very principle of nationalism, would determine the fate of the German people and, indeed, that of the very planet. A Jewish victory would mean not only the end of all culture but, if the Aryan race came to disappear, also the death of the planet. This catastrophe was a theme to which Hitler repeatedly returned. The man's imagination was in thrall to the idea of the extreme situation par excellence—that of annihilation.

The coherence of this ideology hardly requires further corroboration. Although plenty of points, starting with the definition of race, remained vague, there was nothing vague about its construction and articulation. Many of its ideas were already in circulation, but their combination is striking in two respects.

The first is its so-to-speak totalitarian quality. The Hitlerian ideology was cosmic or at least macro-historical. It encompassed the origin of civilizations and even of the planet. It reduced the whole of human history to a handful of determining elements: the observation of racial purity, a struggle between the various races for the possession of rare resources, and the malignant action of the Jews over the previous two thousand years. And, as if to magnify that comprehensiveness at the linguistic level, it consistently intertwined different semantic registers. We have already noted this with regard to biological, religious, and historical registers; to these, those of art and politics should be added.

It would be a mistake to dismiss this interweaving as the result of confused thinking or simply as indicating a half-baked mind seeking to link disparate areas of knowledge into a single system. Fundamentally, it conveys a totalitarian desire to shut down the world of liberal civilization in which social life is divided between a number of autonomous spheres (art, science, religion, politics, economics, and so on) and to do so in order to revert to the holistic universe of the tribe, with all its exclusivism and brutish morality.

The other aspect of Hitlerian ideology that is so striking is the place of prime importance that it assigns to politics. Hitler's thinking was political. He was preoccupied with the means of realizing his ideology and possessed an acute understanding of what was needed for political action to be successful. Pragmatism was his foremost concern. This can be seen from the importance that he ascribed to a highly organized mass party with a modern propaganda apparatus at its disposal, and to the elaboration of not only an external but also an internal strategy. With perfect clarity, he set out the objectives of his foreign policy and also the means of realizing them—namely, a strategy of alliances. In all these respects he had broken with the *völkisch* anti-Semites of both pre-1914 and post-1914. Skillfulness and fanaticism seldom go together, but Hitler possessed both to the highest degree.

How to characterize his anti-Semitism? On one level, it could be said that it was secondary, just a part of his racism. But in truth it was not secondary at all, for it lay at the very heart of his racism. For Hitler, the battle against the Jews possessed an immediacy and intensity unlike any other. What was at stake for him was existential in the strictest sense of the word.

This anti-Semitism of Hitler's combined all the three variants of modern anti-Semitism: Christian anti-Semitism, through Hitler's "Christian rhetoric" ("By defending myself against the Jew, I fight to defend the Lord's work"); national anti-Semitism, through his presentation of a Germany under mortal threat from the foreign presence and antinational behavior of the Jews; and racist anti-Semitism, of course, for this provided the general framework. This was, in short, a particularly successful example of syncretism, capable of branching out in every direction and producing an at least superficial consensus.

More important, this was a radical Semitism, for it represented the Jews as the negative reverse of the Aryan identity. Hitler constructed a relationship of total opposition that implied a total rejection of not only Judaism but also its poisoned fruits, Christianity and all its avatars, which ranged from liberalism to Bolshevism. The "otherness" of the Jews was exaggerated and exalted into an essential "malignancy." The Jews were not only the authors of a two-millennia-old diversion of civilization that was responsible for the decadence of Germany, but they were also the principal adversary now blocking the Nazi path to power.

None of this was new, although the scale and the systematic character of the incrimination were certainly striking. What was new, however, was that the relationship between Aryans and Jews was structured according to an apocalyptic schema. The opposition between the two races was to lead to a final combat of planetary proportions. This was to be a clash between two ambitions for "universal empire": the one attributed to the Jews entirely fantastical, that of the Nazis carefully nurtured.

This apocalyptic schema was derived from the Christian tradition, but it is not hard to see that the latter was reused in a distorted form. The Hitlerian apocalypse accommodated no divine intervention, no eschatology. This battle for racial predominance was a secular one, of a revolutionary nature. The Jews no longer had any place in the divine plan, except perhaps through the anticipation of their conversion at the Last Judgment. They were set up as the enemy at the heart of a battle conceived to be decisive.

By his reuse of an apocalyptic schema, Hitler set himself apart from predecessors who, for their part, had resorted to a Manichean schema. Edouard Drumont, for example, had declared, "When the Jew is on the rise, France declines; when the Jew declines, France rises"—an antagonistic view, to be sure, even a vision of a "final catastrophe" if nothing was done to prevent this, but not an evocation of a battle to the death that would involve the fate of not only France but the entire planet.

Hitlerian anti-Semitism was thus of an apocalyptic-racist variety. The strangeness of the association of those two terms needs to be underlined. The term racism evokes a would-be scientific approach, connoting objectivity and detachment. It suggests the impassivity of the doctor fighting infection and strengthening his patient, the gardener prunning and grafting his plants, or the animal breeder selecting his livestock. Apocalypse, in contrast, conjures up the figure of a prophet, evokes a metaphysical passion, nourishes an existential hatred, the angst of salvation or annihilation (the latter rather than the former being what Nazism cultivated, it must be said).

That association is characterized by the interpenetration of the semantic registers noted earlier: on the one hand that of the "parasitic" Jews, microbes, vermin, and so on, as listed by Eberhard Jäckel; on the other, that elaborated by Claus-Ekkehard Bärsch, featuring the satanic Jew and the Antichrist. Historians tend to emphasize either one or the other. Most associate Hitlerian anti-Semitism with scientism, while a minority link it more with pseudoreligion or a political religion. But it is important to take equal account of both registers for, as already mentioned, they interact fully. To associate them closely in this way is to do justice to the totalitarian aspiration that underlies the confusion. Hitlerian anti-Semitism implacably scours the entire universe, from the microbe to the cosmos. By portraying the Jews as sub-human microbes on the one hand and, on the other, associating them with the suprahuman devil, it produces an unassailable image of dehumanization.

The association of racism with an apocalypse only operated in reference to the Jews, sparing all the other targets of Hitlerian racism. And, as is not hard to see, it carried with it a limitless potential for violence, for anti-Semitism was further strengthened by being incorporated into a strict racism that not only did not spare its own people but even began by purging them. The virulence of this racist anti-Semitism was then further magnified by its absorbtion into an apocalyptic schema that imbued it with all the fervor that a battle between the principles of good and evil engenders.

We have so far been considering Hitlerian ideology. But what of Nazi ideology? It is fair to say that this manifests a certain pluralism, bounded by two poles: on one represented by the Germano-Nordic and anti-Christian wing of Himmler and Darré, characterized by their vision of the various racially related peoples being brought together within a greater Reich incorporating Germans, Scandinavians, Dutch, and so on; and one represented by Goebbels, who was more concerned with mobilizing the masses around a "socialist" rhetoric. The link between the two sides was provided—as usual, with consummate skill—by Adolf Hitler.

However, a wide consensus did exist among the leadership of the Nazi party. It would have been surprising had it not been so, as Hitler was generally recognized as its theorist and *Mein Kampf* was the regime's bible. It served as a reservoir of maxims that were used in countless school textbooks. The consensus related to four points: (1) the racist idea of the diversity and fundamental inequality of the various human groups; (2) the idea of the regeneration of German society by encouraging the reproduction of its best elements, the purging of those who were flawed, and the expulsion of all aliens; (3) the idea of a special antagonism between the Germans and the Jews, an antagonism portrayed in either Manichean or apocalyptic terms; and finally, (4) the idea of an imperial expansion guaranteed by that prior cleansing of German society.

This amounted to a body of ideas sufficiently consistent to direct political action and incorporating enough agreement for the leader at the head of the party, who held the most radical views, to pull that party in a maximalist direction and if necessary all the way to acceptance of the hypothesis of an extreme solution.

*   *   *

Having noted that the Hitlerian ideology did possess some novel elements, that it was fundamentally radical with a potential for limitless violence, and that it provided the bulk, if not quite all, of Nazi ideology, we must now determine what it was that made it possible for this radical anti-Semitism to root itself so firmly in German society.

Clearly, the crucially important condition was Hitler's appointment to the post of chancellor in 1933. His accession to power was by no means inevitable. It was engineered by a clique of politically shortsighted conservatives at a time when the Nazi wave of popularity was already past its peak. Nor was the consolidation of the new regime a foregone conclusion: the Night of the Long Knives in the summer of 1934, when Röhm's SA was decapitated, shows that Hitler was walking a tightrope. Furthermore, it was not inevitable that he should then, within a relatively short space of time, acquire an autocratic position. Taken all together, these developments, completed by about 1937, were crucial for what followed. They formed the context for the period of peace in which anti-Semitism was progressively diffused throughout German society.

That diffusion, seldom closely examined, needs to be explained. At its peak, the Nazi party had received 44 percent of the poll, and this was at the time of the elections of March 1933, which were marked by the proscription of the Communist Party and the SA's campaign of intimidation in the streets. German society contained sizable subcultures, particularly those of social democracy and the Catholic world, which the Nazi party penetrated only gradually. Even within the Nazi party, the motivation for support varied greatly; anti-Semitism was probably a determining factor for no more than a minority.

Yet, by a few years later, this same society had, at least partially, internalized the regime's anti-Semitism, in its most syncretic version at least, if not its apocalyptic-racist kernel. In other words, it had accepted the idea that there existed a "Jewish question," the solution of which implied at the very least discriminating legislation and possibly the departure of all Jews from Germany.

What is the evidence for this? The regime's police reports indicate so, as do the clandestine records of the socialist opposition, which registered the diffusion of anti-Semitism in circles such as the working class, which had been relatively free of it in the past; also, the weakness of reactions to the Nuremberg laws of 1935, the "Aryanization" of 1938, and the *Kristallnacht* of November 1938 are all indications, although the latter, the brutality of which was exceptional in recent European history, did prompt some mitigated response.

On the whole, the reception of the Nuremberg laws seems most revelatory. These laws demoted Jews from the rank of citizens to that of "people under the jurisdiction of the Reich," thereby introducing into European law a distinction of status that hitherto had characterized only the colonial discrimination between citizens of the metropolis and subjects of the colonies. Yet this considerable change, not to mention the sexual segregation that went with it, gave rise to no serious protests—something that would have been most unlikely only a few years earlier and possibly even in 1933.

It is essential to take this change in people's attitudes into consideration, for without it the genocide could never have been carried out with such efficiency and so little opposition. How can it be explained? One ready-made answer leaps to mind. Once the dictatorship was established, the checks and counterbalances to anti-Semitism disappeared, while, conversely, the new regime benefited from the advantages of legality and legitimacy. Those who had hesitated to allow free rein to their anti-Jewish prejudices under Weimar now felt free to do so, and the rest were intimidated. Furthermore, anti-Semitism was now officially encouraged, whether it involved appropriating Jewish property, seizing Jewish jobs, or simply distancing oneself from Jewish acquaintances. Whatever the circumstances, it was internalized, for people had to find self-justification for what they were doing, and, rather than blame their own cowardice, it was easier to appropriate the "good reasons" provided by the regime. Propaganda was insidiously effective, and the socialization of the young through schools and the *Hitlerjugend,* membership of which became compulsory in 1936, was going full steam ahead.

In such conditions, a society rapidly adapts to exclusion, particularly when those excluded are groups that have long been stigmatized. On this subject the historian Detlev Peukert is probably right when he declares that the "national community" created by Nazism rested above all on the popularity of the measures of exclusion that it had introduced. It is worth adding that those measures constituted the reverse of the efforts at inclusion deployed by the same regime. Both sets of measures were designed to give the German people a new sense of self-esteem.

In any case, it seems clear that the exclusion of the Jews could only function provided it was justified by a whole body of representations in what seemed an acceptable manner. For negative images to be internalized, it was not enough simply for propaganda to purvey them, particularly (and this is the paradox here) when those images related to a population such as the German Jews, which was being progressively marginalized and excluded from any positions that might have afforded it even the slightest power over the society that surrounded it.

Over and above the effects of propaganda and the socialization of the younger generation (although in fact most of those who participated in the genocide were already adult by the mid-thirties), acclimatization to anti-Semitism must have resulted from a more complex, indirect mechanism—namely, an internalization of the Nazi regime's political identity. For it did have an identity, one that involved more than simply negation and rejection. Far from constituting a "nihilism," as disappointed conservatives chose to present it at the time, it incorporated a collection of values that it considered to be "positive" and that oriented its policies. To pick out those values, all we need do is return to the historical schema sketched in by Hitler in relation to the Aryan race, a schema that was, at the same time, a model for the future: Aryan peoples who respected blood purity and practiced selection, and who, as a result, developed such power that they were able to conquer peoples far greater numerically and then use these to construct empires that founded great cultures.

The three key values were health, power, and culture—all three interpreted from a racist point of view and all interconnected. Health was the indispensable condition of power, and it was power that created the culture; power was the main, pivotal value. Unlike the French Republic's triptych, these values were never set up as a slogan by the Nazi leaders, but it is not hard to show that these three values constituted so many polar stars that oriented all their policies. And it is equally easy to show that the Jews, and they alone, represented their exact opposite.

Let us rapidly consider all three values, each one positioned at the center of a network of connected notions. Health is probably the value that may most easily be demonstrated to have oriented the actions of the regime. Health meant on the one hand (racial) purity and cleanliness, on the other industriousness and achievement. The healthy, clean, hardworking, athletic Aryan man, married to a woman of the same race who produced many children for him, was set up as a model and a norm. Anything that deviated from this model was, by contrast, thrown into relief and soon became the object of measures of extirpation: Germans suffering from hereditary diseases (about 400,000 of them) were sterilized; tens of thousands of "asocial" individuals and homosexuals were sent to concentration camps; Gypsies were segregated, and so on.

In this situation, the Jews were one target among many others, and up until 1941 the regime's most radical measures affected other groups, since those suffering from hereditary diseases were already being sterilized, and from 1939 on, the handicapped were murdered. The Jews, however, were directly and strongly affected at the level of how they were perceived. The effect of all the regime's measures in the domain of work and health was to reactivate and reinforce the whole baggage of negative images with which they were connected: images of the Jews as parasites, opposed to productive "German work," or, in the register of hygiene, the ancient association of Jews with filth and the whole re-

cent panoply of metaphors referring to the "Jewish microbe" and the "Jewish cancer" that had invaded anti-
Semitic discourse since the end of the preceding century.

Power, as a value, for its part included both the theme of
the Reich—the empire—and that of popular unity. The importance that the Nazi regime attached to power is unmis-
takable. Its propaganda projected the image of a country
bent on reconquering the status of a great power, and the
first stage in this project was rearmament. The new Wehrmacht was the object of a cult, as was conscription when it was
reintroduced in 1935. Both were sources of pride for a people humiliated by Versailles, and were the instruments for
creating a new greatness. But the precondition for any external action was internal unity, an objective that was achieved
through a mixture of persuasion and terror. This was perfectly illustrated by the Nuremberg rallies: with their theatri-
cal settings, they projected far beyond the boundaries of
Germany the impression of a German people welded together around their supreme leader.

If the Jews were one target among others in the case of
health, here they were positioned center stage, for the Nazi's
desire for power, as if in a mirror image, lent growing importance to the clichés that had been crystallizing around the
power of the Jews ever since their emancipation. The power
of "Jewish gold" had never ceased to be a successful theme.
In politics, the Jews' identification with, first, liberalism,
then socialism and communism, had become solidly im-
planted. The association with Bolshevism had even become
the object of renewed propaganda since the outbreak of the
Spanish civil war, and it was compounded by the theme of

the "Jewish war," a war financed by Jews or fomented by them. This was a theme popularized by the German extreme Right in the immediate aftermath of World War I and later vociferously taken up by the Nazi regime, which propagated an image of Jewish power endeavoring to unite the world against the Reich so as to block the latter's legitimate march toward power. This was the context in which the opposition of those two ambitions for "universal empire" found its strongest expression at the level of representations.

Finally, the value of culture encompassed in the widest sense culture both in the common sense of the term and as religion, both of which served to bind the members of the community together. There is no need to dwell on the Nazi regime's cultural pretensions. They were marked by not only a brutal purging of artistic and intellectual life but also an attempt to encourage conformity with the aspirations of the new masters. The figurative arts and architecture lent themselves particularly well to this end. The importance that Hitler attributed to them is well known. His own plans for the remodeling of the Reich's larger towns testify to his taste for a crushing monumentality that was intended not only to demonstrate the creative capacity of the regime but also to speed the onward march to empire by inspiring the people with confidence and zeal.

The negative reverse of the culture promoted by the regime was, of course, the so-called Jewish culture. In the Nazi mind, "artistic Bolshevism" and Jews were fused, as was shown by the famous 1937 exhibition of "degenerate art," which was a fine example of semantic transition. The works of the avant-garde, identified with the Jews, were assimilated to mental illness by the device of hanging many paintings by mental patients alongside them.

Categorizing religion as a value promoted by the Nazi regime may elicit surprise, but it would be ill-founded. In contrast to its heavy-handed promotion of the values of health and power, the regime in this case tempered the expression of its views with prudence. Hitler remained silent as to his deepest convictions and distanced himself from the anti-Christian wing of the Nazi party, notwithstanding his agreement with it on many issues. On the other hand, he would often resort to "Christian talk," usually (but not invariably) invoking "Providence" rather than "God."

Basically, he tried to adopt a position above both the Protestant and the Catholic confessions and tended to use vaguely Christian references in a bid to plug the gap by which Catholics and Protestants were separated, for, like his *völkisch* predecessors, he regarded this as one of the nation's principal weaknesses. More precisely, he endeavored to encourage the emergence of a religiosity that was superficially Christian but the content of which conformed with a racist canon. Hence his support for the "German Christian" wing, which in 1933 predominated among the Protestants and claimed that its mission was to "dejudaize" Christianity.

Despite rejecting racism on principle, Catholics fell into line with the new regime without much difficulty. Like the Protestants, they were hoping for a re-Christianization of German society. To some extent the Nazi regime responded to that hope with its policy of attacking pornography, prostitution, and homosexuality, not to mention the fact that it had already reduced the defenders of atheism, first and foremost the communists, to silence. Keen observers and ecclesiastical leaders, particularly Catholics, were not fooled but did not have the guts to risk a clash in which their flocks would probably not have followed them.

While Hitler, for his part, indulged in his "Christian talk," he allowed his faithful followers, led by Himmler, to support the diffusion of a Germano-Nordic ethnoreligion that rejected Christianity as being not only infected by the Jewish spirit but also a dire symbol of foreign invasion. By 1939, the *Gottgläubig* movement, to which the supporters of the new religion adhered, had rallied about 5 percent of the German population, a by no means negligible number, particularly as it included most of the members of the SS—a fact that needs to be remembered when one tries to understand their racist and anti-Semitic violence.

In the picture that thus emerges, the Nazi regime appears to have started a widespread religious reinvigoration that ranged in many different directions. The effects of this were bound to be harmful to the Jews, not only because it threw their religious "otherness" into relief, quite apart from the fact that this was increasingly interpreted in racial terms, but also because the Jews had for decades been identified with liberalism, free thinking, atheism, and in general with a "disintegration" and "decomposition" of tradition, including—indeed, above all—religious tradition.

In short, the Nazis' efforts to diffuse an identity designed to become that of the German people as a whole needs to be taken seriously. It is hard to assess the degree to which the regime's values were absorbed by the population and to determine which of those values in particular was the one preferred by most Germans. But there can be no doubt that such an internalization did, at least partially, take place. Otherwise, it is hard to explain the growing popularity that Hitler enjoyed, short of postulating that it could be deliberately dissociated from the policies of the regime that he headed.

It is true that the reception of that Nazi identity was facilitated by a series of factors. In the first place, the successes achieved by Nazi policies both at home (principally the reduction of unemployment) and abroad (the reunion with the Germans of Austria and the Sudetans), both accomplished without unleashing war, seemed to invest that identity with a promising aura. Second, the values of the regime were familiar ones that lent themselves to perfectly benign interpretations as well as to extreme racist ones. Finally, they were soon incorporated into institutions that were directed to apply them in such a way as to strengthen the support for the identity forged by the regime.

Foremost among those institutions was Himmler's specialized apparatus, which combined authority over the police force with the direction of the SS and also became the instrument for executing Hitler's personal wishes. But the role played by many other sectors involved in the realization of the regime's values should not be overlooked. Thus, in the health organizations, the tendencies encouraged by eugenics and racism under the Weimar Republic were by now dominant, as were countless similarly influenced experts in almost every domain: the army—the principal tool for the restoration of power; the business world, which had suffered from the collapse of foreign markets during the depression and now supported an expansionist policy that could bring it the kind of profits likely to accrue from an imperial situation; and the world of culture, particularly the circles that had clashed with the avant-garde movement of the Weimar Republic and also that of the Churches.

Either forthrightly or discreetly, all these sectors involved themselves in the realization of the regime's persecution policy. They did so for a variety of reasons: corporative or personal interests that encouraged them to jostle for advantage in the takeover of Jewish jobs and the spoliation of their possessions; ideological adhesion to the regime; or cynicism pure and simple. As a result, as ideas and practices coagulated at an institutional level, racism and anti-Semitism became more solidly established everywhere.

In the absence of fundamental evidence, it is hard to gauge the relative impact of the various mechanisms involved in the diffusion of anti-Semitism—namely, the openly anti-Jewish propaganda, the racist socialization of the young, and the promotion and acceptance of the regime's "positive" identity. All things considered, the importance of this third factor was considerable. The term-for-term opposition with the Jews that the Nazi identity established either implicitly or explicitly not only made anti-Semitism easier to inculcate, but it also, and above all, made it harder to maintain an attitude of hostility or indifference toward it.

At any rate, the cumulative effect of these mechanisms was to reinforce all variants of Judeophobia: Christian anti-Semitism and religious anti-Semitism generally, as noted earlier; national anti-Semitism, as is clearly shown by the ac-

ceptance, without noticeable protest, of the 1935 abrogation of citizenship and the 1941 abrogation of nationality
for German Jews; and finally, racist anti-Semitism, which
grew increasingly strong and infiltrated the two other variants, although in its apocalyptic form it probably affected no
more than a minority of people.

Obviously, the German people were not transformed into
a people of radical anti-Semites, for these remained a minority, albeit a powerful one. However, they did become affected by a Judeophobia that assured the regime of a
sufficiently wide consensus regarding its policies, as is indicated by the fact that the Germans accepted a whole string of
increasingly rigid measures ranging from the 1933 exclusion
of Jews from public functions to regulations that banned
them from engaging in any form of economic activity, a
measure that had reduced them to the state of pariahs by the
eve of World War II.

On one point, certainly, the population and the regime
appear to have been in perfect agreement: the image of the
Weimar Republic. This was now increasingly generally identified with the Jews, and that image became more and more
negative as the new regime demonstrated its ability to do
better. On every level, whether that of health, power, or culture, the image projected by the defunct regime was one of
decadence and failure that now had to be eradicated, if necessary by eradicating the Jews responsible.

In a development unprecedented in the history of modern Europe, Germany had become by the end of the 1930s
the laboratory of an experiment designed to create a racist
and anti-Semitic society, and the Nazi regime was pressing

ahead along this path, strengthened by growing, albeit possibly not homogeneous, popular support. The task that remained was to produce the nucleus of a "genocidal community" from within this apartheid society. The war was to make this possible.

3

RESENTMENT AND APOCALYPSE

WE MAY ACCEPT that the political identity of the Nazi regime, with its perverse mechanism whereby its three fundamental values were set in exact opposition to an image of the Jews, became increasingly widely accepted by the Germans as their own identity (so, to be German was to be anti-Semitic). But what still remains to be explained is how it was possible to move on from a policy involving the exclusion of the Jews and their enforced expulsion from the Reich to a policy of extermination for all the Jews of Europe.

This radicalization came about after the outbreak of World War II in 1939. As is well known, this period was initially marked by a succession of lightning campaigns (Blitzkrieg), followed, in the second half of 1941, by engagement in a long-term war on two fronts on a worldwide scale. In parallel, the period witnessed an extraordinary radicalization in practices of violence. These were encouraged on the one hand by the cover that war conditions provided for the Nazi regime, enabling it to pull off a number of faits accomplis chiefly in the conquered eastern territories, and on the other by the savage warfare that accustomed soldiers to the infliction of extreme violence from which a multitude of victims suffered.

We should remember the so-called "euthanasia," the gassing of over 70,000 handicapped Germans that began in the autumn of 1939; the execution, in the autumn and winter of 1939, of tens of thousands of the Polish elite, the aim of this being the destruction of the Polish state and the Polish nation; the murder of at least 200,000 political commissars during the Russian campaign, as well as of Soviet prisoners of war abandoned without food or care, at least two million of whom died in the first months of their captivity; the SS plans for the colonization of the eastern regions, which envisaged the deportation of millions of people, some of which were indeed implemented in the Polish territories incorporated into the Reich; and, finally, the extraordinarily brutal reprisals carried out by the Wehrmacht in the Balkans and the east as early as 1941.

All these testify to the determination with which the Nazi regime undertook to implement its racist agenda in every respect: the elimination from the German people of all those in some way "tainted," the establishment of an apartheid society in the annexed Polish territories and of a racist colonial society in the rest of occupied Poland and the Soviet territories under Nazi control; and the recuperation of individuals of "German blood," even if not of German culture, from throughout Europe.

The anti-Jewish policy, which was part of this racist program, manifested the same radicalization but in a manner at once more widespread and more concentrated: more widespread since it now affected the territories occupied by Nazi Germany and those of its allies and satellites to which, with certain variations, the measures of exclusion, spoliation, and segregation applied in the Reich were extended; and more concentrated since this radicalization affected the Jews more than any other category. The Nazis had killed thousands of Polish Jews in the months following the invasion of that country in the autumn of 1939, but now, starting in the summer of 1941, they murdered hundreds of thousands in the USSR before eventually setting up the technical apparatus designed to destroy the entire Jewish population of Europe.

Radicalization thus turned into extermination, and it should be emphasized that this happened at a time when other projects in the Nazi plan were actually being suspended, slowed down, or deferred. Hitler suspended the so-called "euthanasia" in the summer of 1941. The elimination of the Polish elite and the deportation of Poles from territories incorporated into the Reich to areas under the General Government was considerably slowed down. Most of the SS's colonization plans remained just that, mere plans, and other policies too were abruptly revised: at the end of 1941 Hitler decided to put Soviet prisoners of war to work instead of leaving them to perish.

But where the Jews were concerned, the needs of the war economy and all the other pragmatic considerations were ignored. The Jews had to be murdered within a limited space of time, before the end of the war. Nevertheless, their special treatment should not obscure the importance that a general racism played in the deployment of anti-Semitic violence. Habituation to violence largely resulted from the actions taken against other categories of individuals. The method of gassing was invented, so to speak, for the killing of the handicapped, and only later was it applied, in a modified form, to the Jews. Similarly, the practice of mass deportation was first tried out at the expense of the inhabitants, Jew and non-Jew alike, of the Polish territories incorporated into the Reich.

Compounded by the brutalizing effect of warfare, habituation to the use of these methods dulled any humanitarian scruples possessed by those who employed them and produced a regression in the process of civilization. It was a regression initiated, even before the war, through the indoctrination of the members of the SS and above all of the security apparatus into which Himmler strove to instill the tribal type of morality (of "toughness") that, as we have noted, Hitler regarded as an ideal. Ever since the Polish campaign, a murderous vibration had been detectable throughout much of the superstructure of the regime. The war unleashed the murderous potential that had been latent up until then and the full force of which was as yet unpredictable.

Why was the violence against the Jews in no way suspended or attenuated? Given the lacunate state of the documentation and the enormity of the event, there can be no certain answer to that question, and historians have, naturally enough, preferred to fall back on the policy of persecution (the role played by Hitler, the interaction of various regional situations, and the desire at the summit to find a "final solution to the Jewish problem") rather than reply to a seemingly central twofold question: In the first place, what did the extermination of the Jews mean to the Nazi leaders? What supreme degree of importance did they ascribe to this undertaking that they wished to keep secret and that they knew represented a transgression of the civilization in which they had been raised, a civilization that remained the framework of reference for many of their compatriots? Second, what was it that, among the German people as a whole, can have disarmed and neutralized virtually all reaction against this radical policy?

As a starting point, let us take the speech that Hitler delivered to the Reichstag on January 30, 1939, on the occasion of the annual commemoration of his accession to power. In it he referred to the extermination of the Jews that would come about in the event of a new world war breaking out. That famous declaration has often been analyzed in order to detect any seed of a policy or any intention or resolve that Hitler might have harbored to exterminate the Jews. Let us now explore it from the angle of the representations and implications that it carried.

In his speech, Hitler declares, "Today, let me once again be a prophet: if international Jewish finance in and outside Europe again succeeds in plunging its peoples into a world war, this will result in, not the Bolshevization of the earth and victory for Judaism, but the certain extermination of the Jewish race in Europe!"

Although the term "extermination" is equivocal, what Hitler had in mind was clearly a physical extermination. His meaning is made all the more clear by the fact that shortly before, in this same speech, he had mentioned another possible "solution to the Jewish question"—namely, the transportation of the Jews to some distant location. It is also important to note that the hypothesis of extermination is presented in a conditional form: if there is a world war, then the Jews will be exterminated. We should note too the somewhat incomprehensible, at first sight, slide from finance into Bolshevism. But for Hitler, those were two modalities and two stages in the Jewish plan to conquer the world, with Bolshevism the very last stage, when Jewish domination would be imposed openly and in all its cruelty. The point to underline is that it is to Jewish finance that the responsibility for the possible world war is implicitly attributed. In other words, Hitler was envisaging a war breaking out in the West, a supposition that was logical enough at the time of his speech.

What meaning should be given to that declaration? The most immediate interpretation is that it was intended as a message for English and American Jews at a moment when the expansion of Nazi Germany was making a European conflict increasingly probable and an American intervention a distinct, though not immediate, possibility. (Hitler had been exceedingly riled by the evolution of Roosevelt's policies over the preceding months.) The message was intended to be dissuasive, maintaining, as it did, the attitude assumed by the German extreme right in the aftermath of World War I, which favored treating the Jews as hostages or as the potential object of reprisals in the event of another external conflict—in other words, a new "Jewish war." This possibility of hostage-taking and reprisals now took on exceptionally wide implications.

A hypothesis of extermination evoked by a state leader is a sufficiently rare occurrence in international politics for it to make a striking impact, especially if proposed within such a solemn setting. That solemnity was further accentuated by Hitler's donning of the mantle of a prophet. His role here suggested a religious rather than a political register and was one that the Nazi leader had seldom adopted explicitly in the past, despite his taste for pronouncements about the future, such as his reference to a "thousand-year Reich." Hitler was deliberately taking up a position of major significance.

Between the political message and the prophetic role there clearly existed an element of tension. If a declaration designed to be dissuasive is to be effective, there must not be the slightest doubt that whoever is evoking the threatening eventuality is ready to bring it about. However, as his use of the passive voice indicates, Hitler was, precisely, refusing to assume such an actor's role. The annihilation of the Jews of Europe would come about, but the action had no agent.

That rhetorical choice of Hitler's clearly reflects a tactical concern: he wished to distance himself from a threat which, if made directly by himself, could not fail to provoke unfavorable reactions, not only abroad but in Germany too. This form of discourse was one frequently used by anti-Semites: violence would be evoked, but no personal responsibility would be assumed for it. A good example is provided by the rhetorical evocation of the "popular wrath" that could be unleashed upon the Jews if such or such a measure were not taken. At a deeper level, such rhetoric is well suited to the prophetic mode, for a prophet is not someone who can bring about the future that he prophesies (in this respect, Hitler is, of course, a false prophet), and the prophetic genre, in its turn, is well suited to the narrative schema of the message that is transmitted—namely, that of an apocalypse.

In his pronouncement of January 30, 1939, Hitler elaborated a condensed and emphatic form of expression for the apocalyptic schema that structured his anti-Semitic ideology as opposed to his racist ideology, in which the former was embedded but which, for its part, was not apocalyptic but simply antagonistic (that is to say, founded upon the idea of a perpetual struggle between the races, but not one in which the destiny of the world was at stake).

The word "apocalypse" means revelation, as of a final battle upon which the fate of humanity depends. The one who discloses this revelation is a prophet, and this is the role that Hitler took upon himself. When he imputed the responsibility for an eventual world war to the Jews, he was reverting to the theme of a "Jewish war," a war fomented by the Jews, which was one of the new themes that modern anti-Semitism had introduced. But he magnified this by inserting it into an apocalyptic schema. He spoke of a struggle in which what was at stake was far more than the fate of Germany. In fact, he did not even mention Germany; rather, he spoke of the world, the Bolshevization of the whole world.

Hitler was, quite literally, a prophet of doom. When, in the same speech, he evoked an alternative possible "solution to the Jewish question"—namely, concentration in a faraway territory—he did not clothe himself in the mantle of a prophet. But, as he had already indicated in *Mein Kampf,* he certainly was a man whose imagination was magnetized by extreme solutions. On that January 30, he revealed that he was ready, in advance, to respond to an extreme situation with extreme measures.

Exactly what kind of situation did he envisage that could lead to the extermination of the Jews of Europe? It is noticeable that he abstained from making a pronouncement on the identity of the victor in any world war. According to his ideology, the future was one of struggle, the issue of which was not predetermined. As the negative construction of the second part of his sentence underlined, he wished to announce that in no circumstance would the war end in victory for the Jews.

In the event of Nazism emerging victorious, it went without saying that the Jews would be eliminated, by what means nobody knew, but probably by extermination or removal to some distant territory, possibly through some international operation. Clearly it was not this hypothesis that led Hitler to play the prophet. Rather, it was the hypothesis according to which Nazism would not emerge victorious, either with the war dragging on and leading to a general exhaustion or, worse still, with it ending in total defeat of Nazi Germany.

If we accept this interpretation, it would seem that what Hitler was announcing was that, even if it was not within his power to decide on a victorious end to a possible world war, it would be within it at least to make sure that the Jews would not emerge as victors. What was virulently detectable in Hitler's speech was the traumatism of 1918, in every respect the historical matrix of Nazism, the point of origin of its ultimate aspirations and its group mentality. A German nonvictory or even a German defeat was a possibility, but a new victory for the Jews was certainly not. Anticipating a world war, an event that his own expansionist policies rendered probable, Hitler voiced the hypothesis of retribution and did so in a way that expressed all the force of his morbid fantasies.

The same line of reasoning is detectable in another declaration that he never tired of reiterating from September

1939 onward, after the outbreak of war in Europe. He repeatedly claimed that Germany would never stand for another November 1918, another capitulation. As in his "prophecy," Hitler concentrated on the worst hypothesis, that of a Nazi nonvictory or defeat, but asserted that he would always retain the power to refuse to recognize defeat, even if it meant allowing Germany to be destroyed and destroying himself.

One more observation about Hitler's "prophecy": the Jews of the whole world were to him a threat to humanity, but not all of them were to pay for triggering a new world war, only those that Hitler reckoned he could reach and that he specified—namely, the Jews of Europe. What he allowed to be glimpsed here (and what historians have generally failed to notice) is that his "final solution" would actually be no more than a partial solution, a second-best: a second-best because it was not in his power to deal with the Jews of the whole world as the apocalyptic structure of his anti-Semitism demanded, and as, we may be sure, he would have preferred to do.

Quite apart from the interpretation given to that declaration of Hitler's, we need to determine what were the functions of his adoption of the role of a prophet. As well as the tactical function already mentioned, two others seem important. The first of these was of a statutory nature. The role of prophet was very familiar in Christian culture and it was intended to reflect and confirm the exceptional aura of Hitler—in other words, his charisma. As he announced the end of a reign (that of the Jews), the Nazi leader presented himself as a medium linking the world of mortals with the world above. In so doing, he surrounded the Jews' fate and his own with a meaning that endowed the situation with a cosmic dimension and an almost suprahistorical significance. Even if it came to the very worst he would at least have raised through those solemn words a mausoleum in which posterity could commemorate the Germanic hero who succeeded in consigning his worst enemy to the tomb before himself succumbing.

The second function of Hitler's adopted role as prophet was to convey a lesson with an associative purpose. Hitler was presenting to those loyal to him and to the German people as a whole his own interpretation of a reality in gestation, a world war that would probably eventually come about as a consequence of his own policies but the responsibility for which he rejected in advance, ascribing it to the Jews. He was presenting that war as a fight to the death against them. By expressing his apocalyptic vision in this spectacular fashion, he was encouraging the adoption of the most potentially violent form of anti-Semitism imaginable. The Germans were being invited to step beyond the national space regulated by the rules of law, even if this involved an exclusion law that discriminated against a minority. But they were being invited to do so not in order to move into the space of interstate warfare, where a number of legal rules were still recognized. Instead, it was in order to move into the metaphysical space of a confrontation between good and evil that could countenance no truce, no compromise, no limit to the exercise of violence.

In short, Hitler was in his prophecy encouraging the formation of a community in which thought and action was unanimously shared, an "interpretive community." He wanted others to share his vision of an extreme situation, and that vision was supposed to extend the limits of what was thinkable, orient expectations, and, if necessary, provide justification for the action taken.

One last element, which has attracted little attention but is just as important, needs to be included in this analysis if the "prophecy" is to be given its full meaning. Hitler had declared just before the cited passage,

> In the course of my life I have often been a prophet and have usually been mocked for it. At the time of my struggle for power it was the Jews in particular who scoffed at the prophecy according to which I would assume the leadership of the state and of the entire people and, among other things, would bring the Jewish problem to a satisfactory conclusion. I think that the echoes of the laughter of those days are now sticking in the gullets of the Jews.

Then he went on to say, "today, I wish once again to be a prophet . . ." In his speeches in 1939 and 1940, Hitler at various times introduced variations on this theme of the ridiculed hero. Casting back to the time when he was an as yet unknown, fighting to save Germany, he stressed that he had often been insulted and mocked. By whom? Probably by Jews. Where his prophecies were concerned, it was certainly they who scoffed at him. The mocking laughter that he ascribed to them was a symbol of their past power. Confident in their strength, they had laughed in the faces of the Germans, laughed scornfully, just like the devil with whom a long Christian tradition associated them.

This image of the all-powerful, scornful Jew who, however, was soon to have the smile wiped off his face, clearly contained an element of sadism. Power had now changed hands; those powerless yesterday were in power today and could ram the laughter of their erstwhile adversaries down their throats. Behind this hate-laden sadism can be detected an aspiration that had not been satisfied by reducing the German Jews to impotence, for now, on the horizon, the power of worldwide Jewry was rising, along with the specter of another world war. That desire was to make someone or some people pay for the impotence of the past, the humiliation—whether personal, social, or national—for which the Jews were held responsible. But what Hitler was also expressing was a resolve never to relive that experience, never to fall back into that impotence and humiliation, never again to hear the scornful sniggers of the Jews: a fierce resolve to prevent that laughter from ever being heard again.

This image of Jewish laughter that was about to be strangled and stifled expressed an enormous resentment. The word "resentment" here refers to an element in a mind-set that was characteristic not just of Hitler but of the entire Nazi group and also of much of German society—a point to which we shall be returning. (It is worth noting that, according to official Reichstag minutes, Hitler's "prophecy" was received by "prolonged waves of applause," a fact that speaks loud and clear about his audience's receptivity.)

Resentment is a sense of injustice, of being in the right and yet mocked, accompanied by an awareness of impotence as a result of which one becomes obsessed with the memory of all the unfairness suffered. But such an obsession may in some circumstances—Nietzsche's analysis springs to mind—introduce a transmutation of values, whereby one may assign a negative quality to that which one has previously desired yet which has remained unattainable. One does this in the name of a new set of values, antithetical to one's earlier set, and doing so can restore a positive sense of self-esteem.

If ever resentment resulted in such a transmutation of values, it happened in Hitler's case, for here was a loser who discovered a new basis for self-esteem in an ideology that exalted the creative power of the Aryan race. The same could be shown to apply to the Nazi party generally, for its chief political offering and the principal source of its success at a time of great crisis was, so to speak, the projection of a refusal to accept humiliation, on the one hand, and on the other an image of "existential power" (to borrow the expression that Eric Voegelin has used precisely of the figure that Hitler aspired to embody). When the Nazi leader associated his role of prophet and the image of Jewish laughter, he betrayed the depth of this resentment, both individual and collective, and also its eminently destructive character.

Resentment and apocalypse are what can be deciphered in the declaration of January 1939. Had that been an isolated and inconsequential pronouncement, it might have been taken as the words of someone hallucinating. However, as what followed was to show, it in fact expressed a coherent thought of a man fully aware of what he was doing.

After the outbreak of European war in September 1939, the Nazi regime continued to pursue its anti-Jewish policy, the aim of which was the Jews' departure from the Reich.

This was partially effected by the emigration that continued until October 1941. Simultaneously, the Nazi regime started to think of mass transplantation to Madagascar in the summer of 1940 following the defeat of France, and then, once preparations for the Russian campaign began, to the depths of the USSR. Had these projects been carried out, they would, at the very minimum, have decimated the Jewish populations of Europe.

As was logical enough, that policy did not envisage any immediate extermination. At this point the international situation and the military position of the Reich did not bear out the hypothesis that lay at the heart of the "prophecy"— that of a worldwide war that might play into the hands of the Jews. However, from the summer of 1941, with the Soviet resistance and the United States drifting toward war, the situation changed. Now Hitler's public speeches as well as his private pronouncements revealed that his sights were increasingly set on the Jews, who were considered to be ultimately responsible for everything that was happening. By the time of Germany's declaration of war against the United States, the apocalyptic reading of the situation, which had until then been kept in the background, seemed fully validated. The Jews had now become the global enemy, conspiring in London, Moscow, and Washington to destroy Nazi Germany.

From October 1941 onward the German press relayed this reading of the situation, doing so the more insistently as Hitler took to reiterating his "prophecy" at short intervals. Since January 1939, he referred to this only once, in January 1941 (although it was dated to September 1939, a mistake

that indicates the central role played by the war), but in 1942
he repeated it in an almost identical formulation at least five
times, and then twice more in 1943. On several occasions he
also reverted to the theme of that Jewish laughter. On September 30, 1942, he declared, "In the past, in Germany, the
Jews laughed at my prophecy. I do not know if they are still
laughing today or if their desire to laugh has already passed.
Right now, however, I can assure you that it certainly will
pass." And five weeks later, on November 8, 1942, he said,
"As a prophet I have always been mocked. But out of all
those who laughed then, countless masses are no longer
laughing today, and those who are may very soon not be."

The importance of those repetitions must be emphasized.
At a time when many people listened to the radio in family or
other groups and when newspapers were avidly read, it must
have been hard not to come across Hitler's "prophecy." (It
was also front-page news in the papers of occupied France.)
This does not mean to suggest that the Germans who read
or heard it necessarily meditated upon it, weighed it, or ap-
preciated its full significance. It only indicates that it would
be hard to imagine greater publicity and it is unlikely that it
was not noted, albeit briefly, by a large proportion of Germans.

Hitler's pronouncement incorporated elements (the role
of the prophet, the prophetic genre, and the apocalyptic
schema) that were both familiar and served to underline
what was existentially at stake in the war. Repeated at the
very time when the extermination was being carried out, it
offered, in an allusive form, a justification, a confirmation,
and encouragement to those executing the extermination

and to other zealots, not only in Germany but also in allied or occupied countries. For those who were attentive and could understand, it signaled that the regime was burning its boats and would fight to the very last. The prophecy thus became a means of implicating all the Germans in what was happening, for although it certainly remained very vague, only those determined not to understand could fail to see that the fate of the Jews was to be as exceptional as Hitler's way of speaking of it.

*   *   *

Let us return to the problem of the meaning that the actors at the time ascribed to this genocide. The foregoing analysis of Hitler's prophecy has shed some light on this by revealing the importance of the value of "power." Given that this constituted the pivot of the political identity of Nazism—health being the necessary condition for it and culture being the expected result—it is clear that, as early as January 1939, the claim that a Jewish force threatening to foment a world war was endangering the success of the project to extend German power was bound to elicit a violent response. As we have seen, the logic behind that response was that it was necessary at all costs to prevent the Jews from gaining a possible or even a probable future victory. Given that "blood" was perceived as the receptacle of the race's full potential, the German losses in a continuing war called for the shedding of Jewish blood too.

But it was not just a matter of "power." Since the Jews were represented as the antithesis of the Nazi on all three

counts, it is not surprising that the other two values were
also invoked in support of the mass murder, albeit in different ways by different actors.

For Hitler's part, his confidences to a small circle of inti-
mates during the period stretching from the autumn of
1941 to the spring of 1942 contain noteworthy references
to the two other panels in the triptych. The prophet had not
entirely eclipsed the doctor, and even if the health theme appears relatively rarely, it is expressed in a striking manner
when it does. On January 25, 1942, Hitler, speaking of the
genocide, explained that if you wished to extract a tooth,
there was no point in easing it out millimeter by millimeter.
You had to pull it out with a single tug; the pain would pass
and health would return.

The theme of culture, in the widest sense, appeared more
often in his pronouncements. At the turn of 1942, Hitler on
several occasions attacked Christianity and the churches,
speaking of his intention to destroy them after the war. This
spirit of hostility is striking, for nothing of the kind is documented in the prewar period. At the same time, Hitler
wanted to plug the gap that would be left by the destruction
of Christianity. He broached the idea of astronomical obser-
vatories that Germans would visit in order to admire the universe and do homage to divine nature. He even spoke of
dictating a short gospel that could serve as the foundation of
the substitute religion.

These pronouncements, which were made in private,
constituted part of the kernel of Nazi ideology. In public,
Hitler, with an acute sense of what was sayable and what was
not, continued to evoke "Providence" and "the Lord." It is

nevertheless striking that, once the extermination of the Jews of Europe was under way, he felt encouraged to denounce the thousand years of misguided civilization that this extermination would, precisely, bring to an end since, as he saw it, the destruction of Christianity, following on the disappearance of the Jews, would achieve the elimination of, so to speak, "the Jew within us."

It is fair to say that these three themes were interlocked with a daunting coherence. The Jews under Nazi control—some squatting abjectly in the ghettoes of the east, others, in the west, reduced, even prior to their deportation, to the status of pariahs—constituted a rotten tooth which, in order to restore the health of Europe, had to be pulled. Their extermination would at the same time serve as retribution for the obstructions that their "racial brothers" in enemy lands were placing in the path of the Nazi march to power. It would simultaneously open the way for the eradication of all that the Jews, through Christianity, had poisoned in the course of two thousand years of civilization.

Now we can see that the realization of Hitler's "prophecy" brought to light a coherent collection of justifications in which all the elements of the Nazi identity were interlocked, ranging from a commitment to hygiene to a concern for the salvation of civilization, passing by way of a cold vengeance. The singularity of this man, who held huge power thanks to his position at the center of the regime and who, it appears, guided and controlled the anti-Jewish violence from start to finish, emerges all the more clearly when one considers the attitude of his lieutenants. They cannot have failed to be struck by the "prophecy," at least by the first time it was repeated, but a number of indications suggest that even they could only hazard a guess at what it implied in concrete terms and that they still needed to stretch their imaginations.

In May 1940, for instance, Himmler wrote in a memorandum intended for Hitler that the extermination of entire peoples was a Bolshevik method that had no place in the Nazi regime. Just one year later he was at the head of those who carried out the genocide. Goebbels, for his part, learned only in March 1942 of the use of methods such as gassing, and entries in his diary testify to the shock that he felt. Thus, even within the inner circle that surrounded Hitler, we need to recognize the radicalization and apprenticeship that these men had to undergo to accustom themselves to the idea of extreme violence, let alone to its actual practice.

Once they had taken that step, they tended to refer above all to the theme of the "Jewish war" when they expressed themselves on the subject. For Goebbels, it became a matter of protecting German generations of the future, and Himmler likewise spoke of how he and his men were responsible for their descendants. The Jews sought to destroy Germany, so all that befell them was fully justified—not that this line of argument stopped Hitler's henchmen from also adopting a hygienist approach, evoking a "Jewish bacillus" and "Jewish vermin."

For Himmler, as for Hitler, the genocide furthermore represented the means to remedy the misguided orientation of a thousand years of civilization by opening the way that would lead to the destruction of Christianity and its replacement by the ethnoracist religion that he was striving to propagate. It was also an opportunity for him to extend his own power and replace the old elite groups by a new aristocracy of a both biological and political nature, which he flattered himself he was forming in the ranks of his organization.

Lower down the hierarchy, most of those involved in executing the genocide (several hundreds of thousands of individuals, or even more if one includes the soldiers who assisted in the massacres of Jews) no doubt did not have such a wide view of it as did Hitler and Himmler. But it was they—men in the police force and the SS, and civil servants in the occupied territories—who had to become inured to this inhuman violence, particularly when it came to murdering women and children on such a vast scale.

Their actions were clearly prompted by a wide range of motivations: bureaucratic competitiveness, obedience to superiors in the hierarchy, group pressure, personal interest, cynicism, and sadism all played a part as did, to a greater or lesser degree, an ideological dimension. In the case of young soldiers socialized during the immediate prewar years, their assumption of the Nazi identity had already prepared them for a negative perception of the occupied peoples of eastern Europe and the Balkans, and, above all, of the Jews of those regions. On a broader level, the distinction between "superior" and "inferior" races, a biologizing view of society, an exclusive ethnoracist allegiance, and the particularly virulent Nazi variant of anti-Semitism had penetrated the minds of many Germans. There was nothing to stand in the way of a radical treatment of the Jews. On the contrary, there seemed every reason to dispose of them in a high-handed way.

In the rationalizations that surface in the official or private correspondence of those executing the genocide, the theme of the "Jewish war" recurs in many forms, the most common being an assertion that the Jews are "partisans" or the auxiliaries of "partisans." But those in positions of responsibility in the civil or military administration in the eastern regions also produce arguments of a coldly utilitarian nature: the murder of the Jews will liberate housing and make more food supplies available. They also adopt hygienist arguments: the "liquidation" of the local Jewish community is indispensable if epidemics are to be controlled. Behind these arguments lay a simple assumption: the Jews had no right to any existence, and besides, their disappearance was just a matter of time.

The degree to which individuals believed in these rationalizations matters little and is, anyway, impossible to assess. But they did make sense in the context of the coordinates of the regime and thus offered a reassuring legitimation. Without the discourse on health, power, and culture that circulated through all kinds of channels and that had been largely internalized and absorbed, it would have been very difficult for those executing the genocide to justify their violent practices to others or indeed to themselves. Hatred needs to batten on to certain representations in order to be converted into action or to get the memory of that violence accepted after the event. And the appropriation of those representations is all the more likely when one believes that one's own identity and one's very existence is threatened by a civilian population to which it is possible to deny the status of victim by attributing to it the status of enemy.

Beyond the circle of those actually carrying out the genocide, the attitude of Germans generally—their perception
and interpretation of it—is harder to discern. The prewar
persecution of the German Jews was witnessed and heard of
by everyone, and their deportation from the autumn of
1941 onward cannot have passed unnoticed. It is true that
the regime's press rarely evoked all the measures by which
the Jews were being hammered, but it readily provided information about the discrimination and deportations proceeding in the rest of Europe, so the scale of persecution
throughout the continent was no secret. Furthermore, numerous rumors rapidly spread about the firing squads oper-
ating in eastern Europe and later, although to a lesser extent,
about the gassing chambers. At the very least, the German
population was vaguely but undoubtedly aware of the unen-
viable fate to which the Jews were being subjected and also
of the fact that their fate set them apart even amid the suffering that the Nazi regime was inflicting throughout the continent. However, reaction both individual and collective, in
particular on the part of the Churches, remained at best spo-
radic and limited.

So what we have to try to explain here is not how people
such as those who actually executed the genocide became inured to violence, but rather how German people generally
were induced to turn their backs on civilization or, put another way, how even their interest in what was happening
became atrophied. This switch-off of interest, an active procedure, is likely a more accurate diagnosis of the situation
than mere indifference, for the German people must have
moved positively to exclude the Jews, including the German

Jews who were their compatriots, from their trust and must have decided that the link of civic, national, or even just human reciprocity that had, after all, existed in the past was now null and void. In consequence, even the deportation of the Jews did not merit the reaction that had at least been expressed at the treatment of the handicapped. This switch-off of interest, which had begun in 1933, became more pronounced after the war broke out, although even then it was not altogether general, as the diary of Victor Klemperer testifies.

It is true that the regime had ways of punishing all gestures of undesirable solidarity. It is also true that, from 1940 on, it backed up its propaganda by a massive diffusion of the first large-scale anti-Semitic cinematographic productions— *The Jew Süss*, and *The Eternal Jew*—not to mention the pronouncements of Hitler, which acclimatized his audience to the idea of a radical solution to the "Jewish question," a solution whose reality was at once covert yet suggested.

All the same, the organs of the regime noted that their propaganda produced relatively little response. The Germans were disinclined to express their views on the subject, which, however, does not necessarily mean that they disapproved. It seems clear that, quite apart from "moderate anti-Semitism," truly Nazi anti-Semitism was now affecting an increasing number of people. What other explanation can there be for the fact that, in December 1941, Protestant churches in Germany publicly justified their decision to ban their faithful of Jewish extraction from their services?

It seems certain that, after the beginning of the war, the Nazis persuaded most Germans that the "Jewish question" had to be resolved and that the Jews' departure was the best solution. It also seems that, in consequence, they won quite wide acceptance for the idea that Jews in general were if not entirely responsible for the war, at least held a measure of responsibility for it. The position that the Protestant churches adopted was thus justified by the argument of the "Jewish war" that had been imposed upon Germany. From 1943 on, the population frequently expressed the view that the Allied bombing raids were designed to make the Nazi regime pay for the treatment it inflicted upon the Jews. All of this tends to testify not only to a widespread awareness of the mass murders but also to a belief in the worldwide power of the Jews and the theme of the "Jewish war," even if the latter was presented as resulting from Nazi policies.

What can be the explanation for the acceptance of fantasies such as these? Once again the mechanism at work seems to have been indirect, in that it was conditioned by the acceptance of the Nazi identity as the national identity—an identity now threatened by a war attributed to the Jews. More fundamental, however, was that acclimatization to these fantasies was made possible by the fact that many Germans were psychologically in harmony with that of Nazism. The reason the perception of the Jews' "otherness" turned into a sense that the Jews presented a threat to the very existence of Germans was that the Nazi regime, and Hitler in particular, right from the outbreak of war managed to propagate a veritable culture of resentment that resonated widely among the population generally.

Hitler's wartime speeches, nowadays largely ignored by historians, display a rhetorical strategy designed to foster in his compatriots the resentment which had been sparked off by the 1918 defeat and its postwar aftershocks, and which, following the few years of calm procured by the Nazi regime, was reviving, laced with added bitterness.

Hitler's speeches indefatigably purveyed a handful of themes that struck one single sensitive chord. They set in contrast to the memory of past decadence and humiliation all the health, power, and cultural creativity that the Nazi regime had managed to restore. They painted a picture of a Germany seeking peace and sympathy, a country upon which an unjust war had been imposed by powers that could not tolerate its renaissance and aimed to destroy not only the Nazi regime but the German nation itself. Such was the theme that they hammered home from the end of 1941 onward. Meanwhile, they breathed not a word about the racist empire that was under construction, the transfer of whole populations that was taking place, the envisaged destruction of entire towns, or the apartheid society in store for conquered peoples.

What these speeches diffused was the idea of a people unjustly attacked, whose merits and achievements were denigrated by enemies who were denying it the very right to exist. And who were these enemies? Countries such as Great Britain, the United States, and the Soviet Union, with which anti-Semites had associated the Jews for years—even prior to World War I, in the case of the first two.

On top of the image of Jews as responsible for both the defeat of 1918 and the abject Weimar Republic came another to be superimposed: that of Jews as responsible for the war then being fought, a war that might lead to another defeat and another Weimar-type experience. The "Jewish Republic" (of Weimar) and the "Jewish War" (World War II) were images that triggered a fatal switch-off of interest. In the end, it was not necessary for the German population to support the apocalyptic-racist anti-Semitism of the Nazi core leadership, or for the German people, like the actual executors of the genocide, to appropriate the "tough" morality that was designed, when adopted, to allow people to kill impassively and thus recover a "healthy" civilization. All that was necessary was for the people to internalize a culture of resentment in which the Jews had played a role of quasi-total negativity. The result of this was to block even a minimum of fleeting compassion for their fate.

*   *   *

As we reach the end of this study, its conclusion will come as no surprise: namely, that anti-Semitism determined the anti-Jewish policy of the Nazi regime and, in particular, its policy of extermination. That is not to say that it was the sole or the exclusive cause, but without it, the massacre would have had neither the initial impulsion nor the perseverance that carried it on to the very end, despite the turn that the war was taking.

To discover the mainspring of that terrible efficacy, we must turn to the structure of Nazi ideology and the mechanisms for the latter's diffusion. This study has underlined the fundamental importance of racism in that structure and the logic of violence behind it that reinforced the grip of anti-Semitism. But anti-Semitism itself possessed an irreducible autonomy that stemmed from its own apocalyptic structure and its position at the heart of that racism. Moreover, thanks to a basic social receptivity far wider than that for racism, the impact of anti-Semitism was far greater then it might otherwise have been.

In that sense, there was an undeniable continuity. Whether it was a matter of traditional anti-Judaism or modern anti-Semitism, the Nazis reemployed more or less every anti-Jewish motif and theme available. Likewise, they faithfully kept alive the radical anti-Semitism of their *völkisch* predecessors, whose Judeophobia had already been constructed as the reverse of the "positive" identity that they wished to implant in their own society and whose values prefigured those of Nazism, albeit lacking the systematic interdependence that Hitler was to give them, with power as their pivot.

Even so, the crucial dynamic resulted from the Nazi's accession to power in 1933. For one thing, the political identity of the Nazis now became that of the regime. The values upon which it was founded took on greater consistency and extended their hold through the interaction of ideas, institutions, and current practices. That same interaction enabled the Judeophobia that constituted the reverse side of the Nazi identity to reach a wider audience and to polarize the other variants of anti-Semitism that were themselves also becoming stronger. Under these circumstances, anti-Semitism came to constitute more than a bunch of prejudices, let alone simply a discourse that was used as an instrument to serve certain material or bureaucratic interests, although it was certainly all that as well. Now, to variable degrees, it became an interpretive grid by which to make sense of what was happening, and it thus became a part of the definition of the collective identity.

Second, precisely because it was successfully diffusing its political identity, the regime created a context favorable to the activation of Hitler's apocalyptic schema, giving him the feeling that, once the circumstances were propitious, his "prophetic" message would be accepted. This would clearly not have happened had not his mode of thought, admittedly in an extreme form, reflected a collective mind-set initially produced by the experience of World War I and its aftermath and then reactivated by the approach and outbreak of World War II. This mind-set, which might be defined as resulting from a combination of brutalization and resentment, existed in a concentrated state within the Nazi party and in a latent state in the German population.

To this extent, everything was interconnected even if the degree of responsibility differed greatly from one individual to another. The familiarity of the anti-Jewish prejudice, the at least superficial absorption of the Nazi identity, the sense of victimization, and the acceptance or attraction of an extreme violence disguised as divine judgment all coalesced to cause a fantastical interpretation of reality—an interpretation that spawned a mass murder that, by reason of both the conditions that allowed its execution and the motivation that inspired it, remains unparalleled in twentieth-century history.

PART II

Fascism, Nazism, Authoritarianism

4

THE SPECTRUM OF ACCEPTANCE

AFTER 1945, WHEN it was a matter of trying to understand the experience of life under the Nazi regime, the word "totalitarianism" evoked for many the image of a society engulfed by an all-powerful authority, as if George Orwell's *1984* had become a reality. With the rise of social history and, in particular, the development of a history of everyday life, perspectives have changed. Now historians tend to draw attention to the boltholes, personal refuges and strategies for getting around the situation or avoiding it—what might, in short, be called society's areas of autonomy. Along with the idea of a monolithic regime, the notion of one with a total grip on power is rejected. However, by overemphasizing the forms of normality that survived, one may dangerously underestimate the deep rupture in the social fabric that the Nazi regime represented.[1]

History "from the bottom" has enriched our understanding of German society between 1933 and 1945 by painting a more nuanced picture and prompting us to seek more subtle interpretations. It has at any rate made it indispensable to query the extent to which the regime's attempt to seize total power was crowned with success. At the same time, however, we cannot resort to a power/society dichotomy and simultaneously argue in terms of an interaction between the two. The Nazi regime, like all totalitarian regimes, sought to win support and to strengthen cohesion, but it could not do this on its own nor could it do so solely by force. Might not society itself have contributed to the totalitarian construction that the authorities were trying to create?

Meanwhile, the regime, for its part, could surely not simply impose its will, for it was obliged to accommodate a civic society that it had not wiped out and that still retained much of its vigor even after the campaign to bring everyone to heel. In other words, German society's support for the regime may, paradoxically enough, have resulted in part or even for the most part from the limited nature of the regime's hold over it.

Nowhere more than in the social domain are historians inclined to underline the composite nature of the Nazi ideology, the vagueness of its components, and the extent to which their application depended upon opportunistic considerations.[2] The situation becomes a little clearer if we define the position from which we are considering it: Are the changes in which we are interested long-term or short-term, and do they take place at the level of structures or of perceptions? For convenience, let us distinguish between two complementary facets of the regime's objectives: the one relating to the structure of society, the other to its cohesion.

In the field of structural changes, we must begin by taking the wide scope of Nazi ambitions perfectly seriously. It was admittedly less wide than in a revolution of the Bolshevik type, since in the case of Nazi Germany the principle of private property remained the basis of the structure of society.

All the same, its scope was remarkable, for the aim, building upon strong demographic growth, was to strengthen the peasantry, reduce the size of large towns, and diminish industrial concentration. In other words, in default of turning the clock back, the plan was to find a way of strengthening a structure overtaken by evolution but judged nevertheless to be healthy and desirable, yet do so without forgoing the advantages of a necessary modernity, if only because of the means of acquiring power that this modernity provided.

It is not hard to spot the disparity, if not the discrepancy, between that ambition and the changes that were actually introduced. In the domain of agriculture, preparation for the war, followed by Germany's engagement in it, speeded up a rural exodus—quite the reverse of the regime's intentions. The employment of women was supposed to diminish, allowing women to return to homemaking and procreation. However, on the contrary, it continued to rise as soon as the possibility of full employment was achieved. It was a similar story with industrial concentration, the technicalization of work processes, the spread of bureaucracy, and the expansion of white-collar workers.

Admittedly, the regime's policy of increasing the birthrate was an immediate success and it was duly fêted as such. However, demographers point out that the increase only partly compensated for the shortfall that had accumulated since the end of World War I. German people, the women first and foremost, intended to decide for themselves on the size of their families, and demographic growth consequently remained far lower than was necessary for the intended colonization of vast tracts of land in eastern Europe.[3] In short, what triumphed were the same long-term tendencies as were currently prevailing in other industrial societies.

All the same, this analysis makes sense only in light of the turn that events in fact took. Through its belligerent expansionism, Nazism caused its own downfall. The fact is that it involuntarily brought about far greater social changes through its defeat than it ever did through all its conscious efforts. It is true, though, that defeat robbed it of the time and means necessary for the realization of its objectives; the military expansion, the racial purges, and social change all went hand in hand. The colonization of the territories to the east was supposed to make it possible to strengthen the peasantry and the middle classes and also to achieve an at least relative reduction in urban and industrial concentration. Despite the limitations imposed by the war, the policy applied in the occupied territories and those annexed to the east do allow one to glimpse the first fruits of a social transformation that, even despite the as-yet deferred expulsion of most aliens and the Germanization of others, did, in the medium term, include a colonial form of society. The major features of this society were the Nazi party's domination, the engineering of a new social structure, and greater opportunities for upward social mobility.[4]

What of the other facet mentioned earlier—namely, social cohesion? This was supposed to be assured by the formation of a racially purged and demographically expansive "popular community" that enjoyed great solidarity thanks to the attenuation of the cleavages (regional, social, and confessional) that divided German society. The condition for achieving this was a Nazi takeover of the traditional institutions of socialization (schools, families, and the churches) and a reduction of social dissidence.

Right from the start, the obstacles were considerable. Past compromises with traditional elite groups and the plebiscitory nature of the regime forced it to maneuver so as not to clash head-on with substantial portions of society. Despite a shift in the relations of the forces involved, the earlier situation persisted and continuity won the day. The continuity of traditional elite groups and the positions held by them was mainly a consequence of the educational system, for this remained selective and was not challenged by the formation of new elite groups in educational establishments controlled by the Nazi party. Upward social mobility continued to be predetermined by origins, educational networks, and family connections. The only exception was the boost provided by political activity within the party, but even this phenomenon remained limited and was offset by a tendency of the old elites and the new to merge. The clearest example is provided by the SS, in which, from 1933 onward, the offspring of the upper classes, including the nobility, were overrepresented.[5]

Cleavages between the Churches also continued to exist and, given the importance of the place held by the Churches in German life, this was at least as serious as the continuity of the social situation. The regime tried hard to bring the Churches into line and to loosen the hold that they retained, over the young in particular. In 1934, the regime even played a part in the institutional organization and theological debates of the Protestant Church, only to back off when faced with the risk of strengthening the current of dissent that was developing among Protestants. From that time on, the regime's policy involved applying pressure and carping; this met with scant success, to judge by the tiny number of Germans who decided to forsake their Church, quite apart from the fact that it was on several occasions forced to beat a retreat when faced with the risk of clashing with the Catholic Church.[6] Religious policy represented a major difficulty for the Nazis (who decided to defer sorting the matter out definitively until the war ended in a German victory), as is testified by the fact that, for administrative purposes, right up to his death Hitler continued to retain his affiliation with the Catholic Church.

Some might argue that, in default of any objective modification of social divisions and the social structure, there was at least a change at a subjective level in the perceptions of contemporaries who, it is claimed, did recognize that greater equality of conditions and opportunity had been introduced into society.[7] However, to judge by regional studies, it seems that, on the contrary, criticism of inequalities remained acute.[8] Not that there were no reasons at all for personal gratification. Living conditions really did improve, admittedly to varying degrees depending on the ability of the various categories to further their own interests, particularly through their professional organizations, and also depending upon the economic priorities of the authorities and the ideological importance that these ascribed to the various social groups.[9]

The workers found themselves in the worst situation, if only because they lost all means of independent defense. However, even their standard of living improved a little, thanks to the short supply of laborers and the consequent abundance of overtime work; and employers did introduce a number of material advantages, such as canteens, changing rooms, showers, and crèches for workers' families. Furthermore, the regime's propaganda was constantly exalting the nobility of manual labor, and, through such measures as the adoption of May 1 as "the day of national work," the regime underlined an interest that even seems to have left some mark. However, all this failed to turn the workers into pillars of the regime, as is testified by the number of demonstrations of discontent in the prewar years,[10] but at least they were not driven into opposition or even marginalized by the regime. A contributing factor was, no doubt, the disintegration of traditional solidarities, in particular as a result of the adoption of a graded system of wages, calculated in relation to performance.[11]

At the other end of the scale was a much-favored group: the bosses, particularly those of big businesses. These were not subjected to any interference in the selection of their business leaders (except insofar as all Jews had to be purged),[12] and they managed to minimize any influence that the Labor Front might have exerted upon the internal running of firms. Business bosses in general benefited from the revival of the economy and the rearmament boom, but also from the discipline to which the workers were subjected, the blockage of wages, and their own co-option into organs responsible for directing the economy. On the other hand, as a group they were neither well enough organized nor sufficiently united to force any changes upon the regime's major policies. All the same, they got the very most they could out

of the situation, including encouraging the regime's policy
of expansion.[13] Some businesses pursued this strategy with
the utmost resolution. IG Farben, for example, involved itself not only in the Nazis' predatory policies throughout Europe, but also in their crimes, by employing forced labor as
well as workers provided by concentration camps, without
the slightest scruple.[14]

The same can be said of German elite groups as a whole.[15]
Their behavior involved a mixture of maneuvering, accom-
modation, and out-and-out participation, although a few
cases of conscience did lead to a severing of relations with
the regime. Some sectors were outstandingly supportive of
the regime, first and foremost the doctors, whose adhesion
to it broke all records. One in two doctors were members of
the Nazi party and one in ten joined the SS,[16] which inevitably increased the chances of their participating in the
Nazi violence.

The fate of the middle classes, wedged between the elite
groups and the workers, was somewhat mixed. White-collar
workers benefited from greater chances of employment in
the private sector, public administration, and the parapublic
sector, particularly within the party apparatus and the administration of recreational policies. Artisans and tradesmen
enjoyed certain measures of protection, but during the war
they were increasingly affected by the priority given to mass-
produced goods and also by the shortage of labor. Finally,
the peasantry, increasingly ill at ease, had to cope with the
discrepancy between the place of honor allotted to it in the
regime's rhetoric and a creeping nationalization of its eco-

nomic activities, not to mention growing difficulties resulting from the shortage of labor.[17]

Faced with a German society that, by the late nineteenth
century, was already becoming increasingly complex, the
regime's attempts to erase differentiations—attempts characteristic of any regime of the totalitarian type—met with serious obstacles, which was no doubt inevitable, given that
there was still quite a wide scope for the representation of
particular interests. Professional associations, rather than
acting as auxiliaries of the regime and Nazifying their bases,
chose to represent their respective clienteles and devoted
their energies to obtaining satisfaction, usually at the expense of other categories.

In sum, a measure of material contentment certainly did
exist, given that contemporaries must have assessed this in
comparison to their recent experience of the economic crisis.
But what of the war years, with all their restrictions, families
torn apart, and the bombing raids? The fact is that, to the
very end, the regime retained a substantial basis of support,
despite a war which, from 1942–1943 on, was clearly going
to end badly. To explain this, let us consider the possibility
that concentrating on the persisting social inequalities may
blind us to another reality: the partial recomposition of a
German identity which, in the eyes of the Germans, made
those inequalities seem no more than one of the many aspects of their situation.

The first factor in that recomposition consisted of the
Nazi Party's efforts to provide leadership and diffuse propaganda, with the aim of creating allegiance or, at the very

least, mass conformism. By the 1920s, the party had endeavored to project the image of a national party that was a miniature realization of the "popular community" to be established throughout the whole country. That purveyed self-image seems to have received a degree of credit and to have contributed to the party's electoral success. After 1933 the party became a huge machine, with close to 2.5 million members; by 1945 that number had risen to over 8 million and to this figure must be added the tens of millions who belonged to party organizations (catering to particular professions and particular age groups of one sex or the other), although it is true that possession of a membership card was not usually the result of free choice.[18]

The vast party machine was run by about two million mini-Führers.[19] A huge circle of people had in this way acquired an importance and power to rival any accruing from money, status, or birth. To be sure, the Nazi Party soon began to lose its attraction and continued increasingly to do so. Nevertheless, we should not underestimate the role that it played in social life through, for instance, the political references that had to be obtained to support administrative requests and that were available through the network of its assistance agencies, not to mention the personal concern for Hitler's well-being that was felt by many individuals. On top of all this, public spaces were constantly invaded by the celebrations that the party organized—truly political liturgies (the annual congress in Nuremberg, for example) that made a considerable impact throughout the country, thanks to the news media.[20]

On at least one group the Nazi Party exercised a decisive

influence: the young. Through the young, it made its presence felt even within families, where its intrusion was somewhat uneasy. All rival organizations were rapidly eliminated, including Catholic Youth Associations that had for a while been protected by the 1933 Concordat. During the war, the party profited by sending many town children into the countryside, where it was able to strengthen its hold over them. Its camps were placed under the authority of the *Hitlerjugend*, which made the most of its freedom from the rival influences of family and school.

The party's influence on the young did not stem solely from these conditions, which promoted its leadership. Young people had their own reasons for accepting its attraction. The regime flattered them, presenting them as the hope for the country's future. The rivalry between the *Hitlerjugend* and school enabled them to play one off against the other, and they (particularly the girls) seized the chance to throw off parental authority. The beginning of a youth culture is detectable here, but this sometimes found other means of expression, ones that, for their part, reveal the limits of the party's grip. For example, during the war, gangs of youths made their appearance in the larger towns, openly—or even violently—manifesting their opposition to conscription.[21]

The second factor in the recomposition of the German identity was the complementarity of certain aspects of the regime's policies on the one hand and aspirations already present in a diffused state in German society on the other: a desire for a society based on merit and accessible to upward social mobility, and also the dream of a consumer society.[22]

The first of those aspirations may explain the sharpness of the criticisms of inequalities mentioned earlier; the second, too, is worth underlining. The Nazi policies for the organization of leisure time, their promotion of a popular car, the Volkswagen; the spread of radio and cinemas; the appearance of television; and the increase in advertising all produced a seductive effect, holding out the promise of an onward march toward a consumer society. By encouraging Germans to react as clients and consumers rather than as mobilized citizens, the regime hardly favored the preparations for war, but it did win a measure of credit that the war did not erode overnight.

The third factor was nationalism. The sense of injustice engendered by the Versailles peace treaty and Germany's loss of the status of a great power, and resentment toward the victors and new countries like Poland, whose right to annex German territories had been recognized in Versailles but was almost unanimously rejected in Germany, were feelings that were deeply rooted, and the Nazi regime was able to exploit and strengthen them. Hitler's successes between 1933 and 1938, rearmament, the remilitarization of the Rhineland, and the annexation of Austria and the Sudetan region were all enthusiastically welcomed, particularly because they had been achieved without the firing of a single shot. In contrast, Germany's reaction to the outbreak of war in the autumn of 1939 was morose. However, the rapid settling of old scores with Poland and France, followed by the attack on the USSR, which was presented as a preventive operation, were perceived as actions not of aggression but of legitimate self-defense against neighbors or powers that refused to recognize that, in the gathering of nations, Germany deserved a place befitting its regained power.[23]

The last factor, finally, was one that overlapped all the rest—namely, the cult addressed to Hitler. The way that the regime was structured, in the form of domination of a charismatic nature, clearly related closely to the attitude of German society, for it was the latter that made the former possible, assuring Hitler of the popularity upon which his preeminence was founded. By projecting upon him widely differing hopes and representations, many of which were a far cry from his real goals, the German population played a crucial part in the construction of the myth of the Führer and also, by the same token, in the dynamics of his regime. This personalization of power was a response to an archaic conception of politics that satisfied a desire for an emotional attachment of a monarchical nature. It operated as a signal: the confidence that individuals invested in Hitler served to indicate that, by the same token, they distanced themselves from the party and the government. The myth of the good king surrounded by bad advisers operated as a safety valve virtually right up to the regime's collapse.

Countless documents testify to the reality of this cult, including studies on the attitude of Germans serving in the armed forces.[24] Hitler embodied national unity and the common destiny of all Germans. He symbolized a grandiose future along with a promise of greater well-being. Plans for the postwar years, proclaimed with many fanfares from 1940 onward, envisaged the construction of social housing on a vast scale and the organization of a social security program.[25] Hitler crystallized all the resentment of a people still haunted by the memory of the humiliation of Versailles and prone to imagine itself to be surrounded and threatened, a chord that he unfailingly struck in his speeches.[26] As the conflict evolved, the fear of police repression grew, but probably not as much as the fear of "Bolshevik hordes." Belief in the genius of Hitler was forced to accommodate a growing skepticism.

Placed within the context of the entire duration of the regime, the people's attitude, which initially ranged from attempts to keep one's distance from the Nazi regime to acceptance of it, soon stabilized, coming down on the side of acceptance. The opposition, in the strict sense of the term, remained concentrated in small groups that expanded as the war evolved. The communists were the regime's most active and determined opponents. Alongside them and the socialists could be found disparate groups of students, high-ranking officials, officers, and landowners.[27] Another by no means negligible section of the population oscillated between deviance and dissidence, particularly in segments in which a minority identity, past experiences, or strong convictions partly immunized individuals against the regime's efforts at penetration. These included, for example, workers faithful to the socialist tradition or won over by communism, and many people belonging to Catholic circles with typically minority reflexes and memories of Bismarck's *Kulturkampf.* Similar groups were to be found in scattered pockets of the liberal bourgeoisie.

The attitude of the majority, however, was one of acceptance—in many cases a mixture of resignation and genuine support and commitment. Thus, the Catholic Church, while expressing dissent on specific issues when its own interests were directly threatened, lavished praise upon Hitler and publicly supported the regime during the war. But what needs to be stressed is the many-faceted character of that acceptance, founded as it was on widely varying perceptions of the nature and ultimate objectives of the regime.

Many of those perceptions were approximative or ambiguous. Rather than regarding the regime as a radically new phenomenon bringing with it violence on an unprecedented scale, German people concentrated on whatever answered their own need for continuity, or responded to aspirations that they considered to be legitimate. And rather than see Hitler as the bloodthirsty and suicidal dictator that he was, they clung to the image of a leader attentive to their deepest longings for peace and harmony—not without some justification, it has to be said, for on several occasions he proved that he was capable of keeping a finger on their pulse and taking their reactions into consideration. For example, after certain members of the clergy had made their opposition clear, he suspended the extermination of the mentally handicapped so as not to compromise the support of the German population in a war that looked like it would be a lengthy affair. The absence of public or official protests from that same clergy at the time of the deportation of the Jews dispensed him from any further demonstration of the extent of his flexibility.

It is therefore not the case that the Germans, clinging to their illusions, played no part at all in what was going on. No one could fail to notice that Hitler's "kingdom" was crammed with excluded and persecuted people. Even if the "popular community" was, for many, more than just a hollow expression, that community was being created in the context of the regime's policies of repression and exclusion, especially when these were in line with traditional prejudices—for example, when it was a matter of getting a grip on Gypsies, "asocial" individuals, or homosexuals, or discriminating against Jews.[28] When the time came for the Jews to be deported and exterminated, many of their compatriots averted their eyes and plugged their ears. Only when the violence exploded in their own streets, beneath their own windows, as on *Kristallnacht* in November 1938, did they manifest some emotion. The regime drew its own conclusions and thereafter took all possible effective measures to envelop its actions in secrecy.[29] In this too, it pandered to a population intent upon thinking only of itself.

There was thus a price to pay for that acceptance. As Martin Broszat has written, the attitude of the German population during the war constituted "a psychological mixture of panic, loyalty, self-pity, and lies, which caused it to be morally blind to the excesses that the regime committed against the Jews, the Poles, and the workers brought in from the East."[30]

NOTES

1. See the exchange of correspondence between Martin Broszat and Saul Friedländer, "De l'historisation du national-socialisme," *Bulletin trimestriel de la Fondation Auschwitz,* April–September 1990, pp. 43–90 (which

first appeared in *Vierteljahresschrift für Zeitgeschichte,* 1988, pp. 339–372).

2. For a general view, see Ian Kershaw, *Qu'est-ce que le nazisme?* (Paris: Gallimard, 1992), ch. 7.

3. See Jill Stephenson, *Women in Nazi Society* (London: Croom Helm, 1975); Claudia Koonz, *Les Mères-patrie du IIIe Reich. Les femmes et le nazisme* (Paris: Lieu commun, 1989).

4. Rolf-Dieter Müller, *Hitlers Ostkrieg und die deutsche Siedlungspolitik* (Frankfurt-on-Main: Fischer, 1991).

5. H. F. Ziegler, *Nazi Germany's New Aristocracy: The SS Leadership, 1925–1939* (Princeton: Princeton University Press, 1989).

6. See Kurt Scholder, *Die Kirchen und das Dritte Reich* (Frankfurt-on-Main: Propyläen, 1977–1985), 2 vol.; Heinz Hürten, *Deutsche Katholiken 1918 bis 1945* (Paderborn: Schöningh, 1992).

7. David Schoenbaum, *La Révolution brune. La société allemande sous le IIIe Reich* (Paris: Robert Laffont, 1979).

8. *Popular Opinion and Political Dissent in the Third Reich: Bavaria, 1933–1945* (Oxford: Clarendon Press, 1983).

9. See Norbert Frei, *L'Etat hitlérien et la société allemande sous le IIIe Reich, 1933–1945;* and Pierre Ayçoberry, *The Social History of the Third Reich, 1933–1945* (New York: The New Press, 1999).

10. Tim Mason, *Sozialpolitik im Dritten Reich. Arbeiterklasse und Volksgemeinschaft* (Opladen: Westdeutscher Verlag, 1977); Carola Sachse, ed., *Angst, Belohnung,*

Zucht und Ordnung. Herrschaftsmechanismen im Nationalsozialismus (Opladen: Westdeutscher Verlag, 1982).

11. Pierre Ayçoberry, *Social History,* thinks that disintegration outweighed integration in the regime.

12. Hervé Joly, *Patrons d'Allemagne. Sociologie d'une 'elite industrielle, 1933–1989* (Paris: Presses de la Fondation Nationale des Sciences Politiques, 1996).

13. See Lothar Gall and Manfred Pohl, eds., *Unternehmen im Nationalsozialismus* (Munich: Beck, 1998).

14. See Peter Hayes, *Industry and Ideology: IG Farben in the Nazi Era* (Cambridge: Cambridge University Press, 1987).

15. See Martin Broszat and Klaus Schwabe, eds., *Die deutschen Eliten und der Weg in den Zweiten Weltkrieg* (Munich, Beck, 1989).

16. See Michael Kater, *Doctors under Hitler* (Chapel Hill: University of North Carolina Press, 1989).

17. See in particular Michael Prinz, *Vom neuen Mittelstand zum Vilksgenossen* (Munich: Oldenbourg, 1986); and Gustavo Corni, *Hitler and the Peasants: The Agrarian Policy of the Third Reich, 1930–1939* (New York: Berg, 1990).

18. See Michael Kater, *The Nazi Party: A Social Profile of Members and Leaders, 1919–1945* (London: Basil Blackwell, 1983).

19. Norbert Frei, *L'etat Hitlerien,* p. 153.

20. See Klaus Vondung, *Magie und manipulation. Ideologischer Kult und politische Religion des Nationalsozialismus* (Göttingen: Vanenhoeck and Ruprecht, 1971);

Peter Reichel, *La Fascination du nazisme* (Paris: Odile Jacob, 1993).

21. See Arno Klönne, *Jugend im Dritten Reich* (Cologne: Diederichs, 1982).

22. See Hans Dieter Schäfer, *Das gespaltene Bewusstsein* (Munich: Hanser, 1981).

23. On the morale of the Germans during the war, see Marlise Steinert, *Hitlers Krieg und die Deutschenn* (Dusseldorf: Econ-Verlag, 1970).

24. See Omer Bartov, *L'Armée d'Hitler* (Paris: Hachette, 1999); Klaus Latzel, *Deutsche Soldaten—nationalsozialistischer Krieg? Kriegserlebnis—Kriegserfahrung, 1939–1945* (Paderborn: Schöningh, 1998).

25. See Marie-Luise Recker, *Nationalsozialistische socialpolitik im Zweiten Weltkrieg* (Munich: Oldenbourg, 1985.

26. See Adolf Hitler, *Der grossdeutsche Freiheitskampf* (Munich: Eher-Verlag, 1941–1944), 3 vol.

27. See Jurgen Schmädecke and Peter Steinbach, eds., *Der Widerstand gegen den Nationalsozialismus. Die deutsche Gesellschaft und der Widerstand gegen Hitler* (Munich and Zurich: Piper, 1985).

28. See Detlev Peukert, *Volsgenossen und Gemeinschaftsfremden* (Cologne: Bund-Verlag, 1982).

29. See David Bankier, *The Germans and the Final Solution* (Oxford: Blackwell, 1992).

30. Martin Broszat, *L'Etat hitlérien. L'origine et l'évolution des structures du IIIe Reich* (Paris: Fayard, 1985), p. 454.

5

A CONGENITAL VIOLENCE

VIOLENCE CONSTITUTED THE heart of Nazism, defining its identity and creating its historical face. In Bolshevism, doctrine and reality were at loggerheads: instead of whittling down the state, it created Leviathan; instead of fraternity, it produced the Gulag. But in Nazism, doctrine and reality were welded right from the start. The cult of heroic virility, the endorsement of the right of the strongest, the rhetoric on the salutary nature of toughness: all show that violence was not only a means but in itself constituted a value, a kind of "law of nature"—in fact the only one able to guarantee survival and victory in the struggle between the races which, according to the Nazis, constituted the very fabric of the history of the living world.

Nazism converted this violence founded on doctrine and exalted in words into action all the more forcibly since its very agenda required this: its plan was to turn German society into a warrior tribe, to conquer the whole European continent and then to remodel it according to racist criteria. Bent on war, the Third Reich was possessed by violence, as it demonstrated first to the German population and then, once war broke out, to the peoples that it conquered, foremost among them those aliens unfortunate enough to dwell inside the "vital space."

Between 1933 and 1945, Nazi violence developed steadily, becoming increasingly extensive and radical: the circle of its victims expanded and the forms it took became increasingly savage. It is not the case that the use of violence remained unchanged from start to finish. On the contrary, it developed as people became inured to it. But if the Nazi ideology and mind-set had not been particularly disposed to violence, this would not have happened with such disturbing ease. To pinpoint the specific elements of this violence, we therefore need to study the reasoning behind it, the actors who put it into practice, and the forms that it took.

*   *   *

It is possible to distinguish three lines of reasoning behind the Nazi violence. Historically, they merged. However, for the purposes of an analysis, it is useful to separate them. The first line of reasoning concerned political repression: all opponents of the regime, both within the Reich and in the occupied territories, had to be neutralized. This type of repression matched the desire for control and change that motivated the Nazi leaders. It took the form of not only attacks against active opponents but also the criminalization of many types of behavior and attitudes that, under liberal regimes, develop in the private sphere and are based on what are regarded as the rights of individuals. In the occupied countries, violence also took the form of terrorist practices that targeted civilian populations and were designed to establish Nazi order.

In the prewar period such politically motivated violence was relatively limited, except in the early months of 1933, when a wave of terror crashed down upon the Nazi party's enemies. About 50,000 individuals were interned in makeshift camps where the SA, in particular, set about settling old scores with great brutality. Then, as consolidation of the regime went ahead and its opponents became increasingly isolated, political repression declined. The population of the concentration camps, which were now all brought under SS control, even flattened out in the mid-1930s (with 7,500 detainees in 1936–1937).[1] But by now the camps were an institution, ready to be pressed into service whenever needed. Throughout the duration of the regime, the repression struck, above all, the members of left-wing parties—first and foremost the communists. From the mid-1930s onward, not even members of the clergy were spared, and these were soon followed by the conservative opposition, particularly in the aftermath of the attempt to assassinate Hitler in 1944.

The same line of reasoning that supported politically motivated repression led to the criminalization of any opinions unacceptable to the regime. Jehovah's Witnesses brought the wrath of the authorities down upon their heads by refusing to do military service. Seditious talk of every kind was punished equally vigorously, especially criticism of Hitler himself or his racial policy. A sword of Damocles was thus suspended above the entire population, particularly anyone who did not conform to the authorities' expectations.

The impact of the rumors surrounding the concentration camps was, of course, considerable, as was that of the actions of the state's traditional repressive organs, which, under constant pressure from Hitler, handed out punishments of an increasingly severe nature to the non-Jewish German citizenry. Between 1933 and 1945 civil courts passed 16,560 death sentences, almost all of which were carried out.[2] Court-martials condemned about 50,000 individuals to death.[3] About 15,000 Wehrmacht soldiers were executed, whereas in the course of World War I only 48 German soldiers were condemned to death and executed.[4] However, what the Nazi Party suffered was in no way comparable to the Stalinist purges. The episode that bears the closest comparison, that of the Night of the Long Knives, in June 1934, when the leadership of the SA was decapitated, claimed just over 80 victims.

The outbreak of war spurred on such repression, above all in the occupied territories. In the name of maintaining order, a process that was given a most extreme interpretation, the Nazi occupiers unleashed what may fairly be described as a terrorist wave of violence in the USSR, Poland, and the Balkans. Eventually, in 1943, this began to recoil westward, but by then it had lost much of its momentum. The number of civilians killed by the Germans within the framework of the policy of collective reprisals is hard to estimate, but it far exceeded the one million mark. Take the case of Byelorussia: out of a population of roughly 9 million, the Nazis, in the course of antipartisan operations, killed some 345,000 civilians, only 10 to 15 percent of whom were carrying a weapon at the time of their deaths. The great majority of these victims were villagers suspected of aiding the partisans or living in areas that the German authorities had decided to depopulate in order to defeat the partisans.[5] As is well known, the brutal treatment of the populations of occupied territories was marked by pitiless economic exploitation that included massive deportations of workers. In all, some 8 million foreigners working under the Nazi whip kept the German war economy turning.[6]

The concentration camps reflected the rising intensity of Nazi repression. They became a Tower of Babel in which men and women of every nation coexisted. German detainees constituted no more than a tiny minority, and received privileged treatment. At the beginning of the war the concentration camp population had numbered close on 25,000 people. That figure had multiplied by four by 1942, by ten in the summer of 1943, and by thirty at the beginning of 1945 (in January 1945 there were 714,211 concentration camp detainees, 202,674 of whom were women).[7] In all, at least 1.5 million people experienced the hell of the camps. Two-thirds of them died there as a result of brutality, exhaustion, or diseases to which they were deliberately exposed.

The second line of reasoning behind the Nazi violence was prompted by the desire for social reform and aimed for the homogenization of the "popular community," or the population defined as German.[8] Not content with indoctrinating the population and keeping it under surveillance to ensure that it conformed with Nazi expectations, the regime resorted to both punishment and exclusion, setting its sights on all those whom it judged to be unwilling to or incapable of fitting into the "popular community." Its main targets were two categories of people: "asocials,"[9] who included Gypsies, vagabonds, beggars, prostitutes, alcoholics, out-of-work individuals who rejected employment, and those who left their jobs frequently or for no good reason, and homosexuals, whose behavior undermined the imperative of reproduction and who accordingly became the object of ferocious repression. The courts condemned about 50,000 individuals for homosexuality, half of them in the short space of time between 1937 and 1939. Once they had served their normal prison sentences, many were sent on to the camps, where most of them died.[10]

The violence directed against these categories, which intensified midway through the 1930s, seems to have been partly motivated by a concern to put unproductive individuals to work at a time when preparations for war were leading to a shortage of labor. More fundamentally, though, it was a matter of ridding the public of types of behavior that did not fit in with the social norms of the regime. Many of the latter, such as the virtues of hard work and discipline, and sexual conformism, in fact met with the approval of a large portion of the population. This policing of mores could be extended indefinitely to cover all kinds of social deviance, as is shown by the mini-war that urban authorities waged against gangs of young people (known as *Edelweisspiraten*), who dressed in a provocative manner, congregated to listen to jazz, and sometimes engaged in fisticuffs with the *Hitlerjugend*.[11]

The third line of reasoning and the most important was of a racist nature. It advocated two kinds of action. One involved restoring the German people to health, the other purging the territories under Nazi control. Where racism is concerned, it is often not fully realized that before being directed against alien populations, it tends, logically enough, to be applied against the racists' own society, the goal being to eradicate all seeds of decadence there. This was the objective of one of the first laws passed by the Nazi regime; it imposed sterilization on all those suffering from physical handicaps or psychiatric or neurological disabilities that were judged to be hereditary by the medical experts of the day. About 400,000 people underwent this treatment, which caused a number of deaths and countless cases of traumatism. In 1937, Hitler extended the law to cover several hundred young Germans who had been fathered by black members of the French troops of occupation stationed in the Rhineland between 1919 and 1930.[12]

This same line of reasoning led to the so-called "euthanasia" operation, which in reality consisted of the serial killing of mentally sick people classed as both incurable and unproductive.[13] Within two years, the operation, launched in the autumn of 1939, had murdered over 70,000 victims selected from among the patients of psychiatric establishments. It was at this time that the gassing procedure was "invented." It took place in a chamber camouflaged as a shower-room and was followed up by the incineration of the corpses and the recovery of their gold teeth—all procedures that were later reemployed in the extermination of the Jews. Five thousand children born with deformities were also killed by injection at this time.

Hitler suspended the operation in the summer of 1941, following protests from members of the clergy. But it con-

tinued sporadically after a switch in targets. About 20,000
sick detainees were gassed in the concentration camps, as
were at least 30,000 Polish and Soviet workers suffering
from tuberculosis or mental illnesses.[14]

The so-called "euthanasia" operated in secret and was ad-
ministered by doctors; it affected individuals whose physical
state reduced them to total impotence, including in the sexual sense. There was thus no risk involved for the authorities:
it was not a matter of repression or terror, both of which
would have presupposed a degree of publicity, but "just" an
elimination based on strictly racist principles. The most base
utilitarian motives sufficed for the assassination of these people declared to be "unworthy to live." It was thus that
Himmler's men murdered thousands of patients from psychiatric establishments in annexed Poland and the occupied
USSR, gassing them in lorries or executing them by firing
squads simply to liberate housing for their own troops.[15]

The second kind of racial purging targeted aliens living in
the Reich itself or in the conquered territories. A policy of
apartheid was elaborated to separate Jews from the "Aryan"
population at all levels, including that of sexual relations (the
Nuremberg Laws, 1935). The policy was then extended to
cover the foreign workers who had to be imported in order
to keep the wartime economy going. The sanctions imposed
against this group were made even stricter, particularly for
Poles. Sexual relations with a German woman rated the
death sentence, while violation of any of the countless prohi-
bitions for workers from the eastern regions—for example,
entering inns or attending German religious services—could
lead to incarceration in a concentration camp.[16]

In the conquered territories of eastern Europe, the purges began with the liquidation of elite groups. In annexed as well as occupied Poland, they claimed tens of thousands of victims before being suspended in response to protests made by Wehrmacht leaders. But in the occupied Soviet Union, the liquidation of elite groups went ahead unchecked, for there, any scruples on the part of the military were cancelled out by anticommunism and anti-Semitism. Soviet prisoners of war were scanned to identify not only Jews but also those who had held positions of responsibility in the Communist Party or the Soviet state, or who belonged to the intelligentsia. Hundreds of thousands of prisoners selected in this way were shot.[17]

In massacring the Polish and Soviet elites, the Nazis' purpose was to wipe out not only the administrative pillars of states scheduled to disappear, but also all individuals with what was now an outlawed political or national identity. At the same time, they set about weakening the national consciousness of the conquered populations, in particular by closing down all cultural and educational institutions with the exception of primary schools and certain technological establishments so as to reduce the people to the state of unqualified laborers, talliable and liable to forced labor at their masters' pleasure until such time as the victors were in a position to Germanize their "vital space" completely.

The ultimate Nazi objective was expulsion. In the annexed Polish territories, deportations began without delay. Out of about ten million inhabitants, roughly one million were deported to what was known as the General Government (the nonannexed part of Poland under German military administration).[18] However, the transport needs of the army later obliged Himmler to reduce these deportations as well as those from Alsace-Lorraine after tens of thousands of people had been sent to Vichy France. But the ultimate objective remained unchanged, as can be seen from the Eastern Plan elaborated in the aftermath of the attack on the USSR in June 1941. This envisaged deporting 31 million Slavs to Siberia and replacing them with 4 million German settlers.[19]

In their efforts to effect such racial remodeling, the Nazis faced one major obstacle: the demographic preponderance of Slavic peoples. Hence the desire, expressed by Himmler, to reduce their birthrate by every means possible, including mass sterilization. The treatment of Soviet prisoners of war was also affected by this demographic anxiety. In the summer and autumn of 1941, close to two million of them died of hunger, cold, or disease within no more than a few months of their capture. True, the German army was not prepared for coping with the upkeep of such a huge mass of men, but that very unpreparedness, in its turn, cannot be understood without taking into account factors such as political mistrust, cultural and racial scorn, and, above all, the intention to reduce part of the Soviet population to famine in order to enable the Reich to siphon off a surplus of food supplies. (Eventually, from the time of the military crisis of 1941–1942 onward, the increasingly pressing need for laborers did offer at least a chance of survival to the Soviet soldiers captured as prisoners of war.)

Another way of reducing the demographic imbalance was to recover those of "German blood" present among the Slavic peoples. The Eastern Plan envisaged Germanizing 10 to 15 percent of the Poles (who would thus be spared deportation to Siberia) and likewise 50 percent of the Czechs, 35 percent of the Ukranians, and 25 percent of the Ruthenians.[20] This Germanization affected people who for the most part had no linguistic or cultural links at all with Germany, but who, following a physical examination, were nevertheless declared to be of German descent. The next step was to acculturate and Nazify them, a process that involved employing means of constraint in recalcitrant cases. Although the turn that the war was taking set strict limitations on this effort, thousands of Slovenians, for example, whom Himmler had decided to Germanize, were notwithstanding deported to the Reich. Similarly, thousands of Polish orphans were placed in German adoptive families.

In the case of certain populations, eventual expulsion no longer seemed an acceptable solution, while Germanization, either immediate or deferred, was ruled out on principle. For the Jews and the Gypsies, the racial remodeling of Europe would one day mean extermination, once other policies such as emigration, deportation, or confinement within special reservations had all been abandoned.[21] In contrast to other victims of Nazi violence, here it was a matter of entire populations—whole families—for genocide can tolerate no exemptions. However, the extermination planned for the Jews retained certain specific, unique features. For one thing, in Nazi ideology the Jews represented a central enemy, so they were both animalized (as vermin, microbes, and so on) and demonized as being under orders from Moscow, London, and Washington; second, their extermination was planned as an operation both global (it included

Jews from all parts of Europe under Nazi influence), systematic (it was centrally organized), and urgent (it had to be completed before the end of the war).

* * *

Political repression, social reform, and racial purging: once again, it is important to emphasize that in historical reality these three forms of motivation merged. But it is patently clear that the racist line of argument penetrated and largely determined the other two: in the case of political repression, the treatment of opponents was much harsher in the eastern regions, where the populations were deemed racially inferior; in the case of social reform, the Nazis increasingly tended to racialize social deviances, attributing them to genetic factors and thereby, at a stroke, felling not only the individuals concerned but also their families, who were all likewise subjected to enforced sterilization.

Who were the actors who took part in this violence superdetermined by racist ideology? There is no need to dwell at length upon the institutions primarily responsible: the police, the SS, the Wehrmacht, and particular agencies such as the Führer's Chancellery, to which Hitler entrusted the murder of the mentally sick. Nor shall we dwell upon the immediate executors of the violence, such as the guards of the concentration and extermination camps and the policemen responsible for the mass shooting of Jews in the USSR and Poland. In all, between 100,000 and 200,000 Germans performed such tasks, aided by thousands of auxiliaries of other nationalities. These men became inured to mass murder, and it is hard to gauge what part was played by ideological motivation, anti-Semitic hatred in particular, and what part by the context—for example, group pressure—and ingrained habits of obedience and conformism.[22]

But over and above those agencies and teams of people, the contribution of the militant kernel of the Nazi Party does need to be stressed. Here, a culture of violence acquired through the experience of World War I had been fueled by the clashes that took place under the Weimar Republic, the attempted putsches in the early 1920s, and the latent civil war of 1930–1933, in which hundreds died. These militants were in the front line in the episodes of street violence that punctuated life under the Nazi regime: in the days following the *Anschluss,* when indescribable humiliations were inflicted on the Jews of Vienna; on *Kristallnacht;* and in wartime punitive actions against both their own compatriots and foreign workers who violated the rules of apartheid.

It is true that they enjoyed the support of a substantial proportion of the population—active support sometimes. Without the aid of denunciations, for example, the Gestapo would not have been nearly as effective.[23] At other times, the support was simply a matter of approval, vociferously expressed at the execution of the SA leaders in 1934 and during the campaign against "asocial" elements, but more muted and ambiguous in the face of the murder of the mentally ill. It should be added that, to the extent that Nazism exploited nationalism and traditional militarism, it implicated a large swathe of German society, beginning with those of the masculine population who served in the armed forces. The violence of the Third Reich derived part of its propulsive force from the manner in which it interconnected all the mainsprings of national violence, doing so with particularly redoubtable efficacy whenever its ideology drew support from deeply rooted prejudice, such as that manifested against Poles, Russians, and Jews.

All things considered, however, the contribution of another group was even more important: that of the highly trained experts.[24] We must not underestimate the crucial role that categorization played in Nazi violence, as it also did in Stalinist violence. The definition of target groups carried out by jurists and other experts of all kinds was an indispensable prior condition for discrimination and persecution. One has only to think of the role that "criminal biology" played in the racialization of forms of social deviance, or that medicine played in the experiments carried out on detainees and also in the process of the extermination of the mentally sick and the Jews. Specialists in the social sciences—geographers, town planners, and economists—also carried considerable responsibility as they planned the racial and social remodeling of the eastern territories, with all its implications of death, either immediate or eventual, for their native populations.[25] A vast range of highly trained experts contributed their skills to Nazi violence. Without them, it could neither have been so all-enveloping nor developed the specific features that characterized it.

This violence took a variety of forms, which we should now, by way of conclusion, briefly note, organizing them according to a public/secret classification. The public category included forms of violence that may be described as popular, even though it was the Nazi Party that deployed or orchestrated them. It was popular violence in the sense that it was aimed against forms of deviant behavior that did not warrant punishment in prison or a concentration camp but that the party set out to stigmatize in a public space, in the presence of onlookers. It was also popular violence in the sense that its methods were borrowed from the traditional repertoire of community violence: an alcoholic would be pilloried or paraded through the streets, with a label tied around his neck; women who had had sexual relations with foreigners would have their heads shaved. Toward the end of the war, this type of violence also turned against foreign workers who were recalcitrant, or simply to make them pay for the foreign bombing raids. Another form of public violence was military or police action designed to convey a specific message. This was mostly practiced in the occupied countries, particularly in the east and the Balkans. It took the form of the burning of villages or public hangings with the bodies left for all to see for several days, and so on.[26]

In contrast, the violence of the camps, which struck at both the body and the spirit, was engulfed in secrecy.[27] There was physical violence, corporal punishment—the usual method of coercing bodies—and there was clinical experimentation, which caused the deaths of thousands of both adults and children. There was also psychic violence; one feature of the Nazi camps, even more distinguishing than their death rate, which was on average higher that that of the Soviet gulag, was the perversity that pervaded the guards' relations with the detainees and that was evident in their efforts to break the spirits of the latter, to degrade them and strip them of their dignity as human beings. One figure that provided an illustration of that perversity was the "Muslim," the name used for a detainee who had sunk to the very lowest level of somatic and psychological decay. Hannah Arendt judged, with reason, that the difference between the Stalinian and the Nazi camps could be likened to the difference between purgatory and hell.[28]

Equally secret were the mass murders perpetrated by the Nazis, whether by shooting or gassing.[29] Both methods testify to an industrial-type rationalization of massacre, accompanied by a dehumanizing representation of the victims, but the gas chamber represented the more advanced stage of that rationalization and, above all, dehumanization. What it reduced its victims to in their last moments testified to an ultimate dehumanization. Whereas death by shooting afforded the martyrs at least the possibility to offer each other a measure of mutual comfort and to feel something like a sense of solidarity in their trials, the gas chamber camouflaged as a shower room ruled out anything of the kind. The sudden darkness provoked terror, suffocation increased this to panic, and families clinging together were swept apart in a wild rush for the door. Next, everyone tried to find oxygen to breathe up close to the ceiling. The strong trampled on the weak—relatives, loved ones and friends no longer mattered. Human beings found themselves reduced to the most elementary of all impulses, the desire to survive, which can dissolve every social link and every last vestige of solidarity and dignity.

NOTES

1. See Martin Broszat, "Nationalsozialistiche Konzentrationslager 1933–1945," in *Anatomie des SS-Staates* (Munich: DTV), vol. 2, pp. 11–133.

2. Eberhard Kolb, "Die maschinerie des terrors," in Karl Dietrich Bracher, Manfred Funke, and Hans-Adolf Jacobsen, eds., *Nationalsozialistische Diktatur, 1933–1945. Eine Bilanz* (Düsseldorf: Droste, 1983), p. 281.

3. Manfred Messerschmidt and Fritz Wüllner, *Die Werhmachtjustiz im Dienste des Nationalsozialismus* (Baden-Baden: Nomos Verlagsgesellschaft, 1987), p. 87.

4. Omer Bartov, *Hitler's Army, Soldiers, Nazis and War in the Third Reich* (Oxford: Oxford University Press, 1991), pp. 95–96.

5. See Christian Gerlach, *Kalkulierte Morde. Die deutsche Wirtschafts- und Vernichtungspolitik in Weissrussland 1941 bis 1944* (Hamburg: Hamburger Edition, 1999), pp. 907 f.

6. See Ulrich Herbert, *Fremdarbeiter, Politik und Praxis des "Auslander-Einsatzes" in der Kriegswirtschaft des Dritten Reiches* (Bonn: Verlag Dietz, 1985).

7. Broszat, "Nationalsozialistische Konzentrationslager," vol. 2, pp. 11–133.

8. See Michael Burleigh and Wolfgang Wippermann, *The Racial State: Germany, 1933–1945* (Cambridge: Cambridge University Press, 1991).

9. See Wolfgang Ayass, *"Asoziale" im Nationalsozialismus* (Stuttgart: Klett-Cotta, 1995).

10. Burleigh and Wippermann, *The Racial State,* p. 197.

11. See Arno Klönne, "Jugendprotest und Jugendopposition. Von der HJ-Ezehung zum Cliquenwesen der Kriegszeit," in Martin Broszat, ed., *Bayern in der NS-Zeit* (Munich: Oldenbourg, 1981), vol. 4, pp. 527–620.

12. See Gisela Bock, *Zwangssterilisation im Dritten Reich* (Opladen: Westdeutscher Verlag, 1986).

13. See Michael Burleigh, *Death and Deliverance: "Euthanasia" in Germany c. 1900–1945* (Cambridge: Cambridge University Press, 1994).

14. Hans-Walter Schmuhl, *Rassenhygiene, Nationalsozialismus, Euthanasie* (Gottingen: Vandenhoeck and Ruprecht, 1987), pp. 361–364.

15. See Götz Aly, ed., *Aktion T-4 1934–1945* (Berlin: Hentrich, 1987).

16. See Diemut Majer, *"Fremdvölkische" im Dritten Reich* (Boppard am Rhein: Boldt, 1981).

17. Current estimates put the figure at 600,000 people executed (see Christian Streit, *Kleine Kameraden. Die Wehrmacht und die sowjetischen Kriegsgefangenen 1941–1945* [Stuttgart: DVA, 1978]).

18. See Jan Gross, *Polish Society under German Occupation: The General Government, 1939–1944* (Princeton: Princeton University Press, 1979).

19. See Mechtild Rössler and Sabine Schleiermacher, eds., *Der "Generalplan Ost". Hauptlinien der nationalsozialistischen Planungs-und Vernichtungspolitik* (Berlin: Akademie Verlag, 1993).

20. Helmut Heiber, "Der Generalplan Ost," *Viertel-jahrshefte für Zeitgeschichte,* 1958, pp. 281–325.

21. See Raul Hilberg, *The Destruction of the European Jews* (New York and London: Holmes and Meier, 1985); Michael Zimmermann, *Verfolgt, vertrieben, vernichtet. Die national-sozialistische Vernichtungspolitik gegen Sinti und Roma* (Essen: Klartext, 1989); see also Ulrich Herbert, ed., *Nationalsozialistische Vernichtungspolitik, 1939–1945. Neue Forschungen und Kontroversen* (Frankfurt-on-Main: Fischer, 1998).

22. See the divergent interpretations of Daniel J. Goldhagen (*Hitler's Willing Executioners: Ordinary Germans and the Holocaust* [London: Little Brown, 1996]) and Christopher Browning (*Ordinary Men: Reserve Police Batallion 101 and the Final Solution in Poland* [New York: HarperCollins, 1992]); the latter seems the more convincing.

23. See Robert Gellately, *The Gestapo and German Society: Enforcing Racial Policy, 1933–1945* (Oxford: Clarendon Press, 1990).

24. See Benno Müller-Hill, *Science nazie, science de mort. L'extermination des Juifs, des Tziganes et des malades mentaux* (Paris: Odile Jacob, 1989); Robert Proctor, *Racial Hygiene: Medicine under the Nazis* (Cambridge, MA: Harvard University Press, 1988).

25. See Götz Aly and Susanne Heim, *Vordenker der Vernichtung. Auschwitz und die deutschen Pläne für europäische Neuordnung* (Hamburg: Hoffmann und Campe Verlag, 1991).

26. See the catalogue of the *Vernichtungskrieg. Verbrechen der Wehrmacht 1941 bis 1944* exhibition (Hamburg: Hamburger Edition, 1996).

27. Wolfgang Sofsky, *Die Ordnung des Terrors: das Konzentrationslager* (Frankfurt-on-Main: Fischer, 1997), Klaus Drobisch and Günter Wieland, *System der NS-Konzentrationslager, 1933–1939* (Berlin, Akademie Verlag, 1993).

28. Hannah Arendt, *The Origins of Totalitarianism* (New York: Harcourt-Brace, 1976). Compare with Gerhard Armani, "Das Lager (KZ und GULAG als Stigma der Moderne," in Matthias Vetter, ed., *Terroristische Diktaturen im 20, Jahrhundert* (Opladen: Westdeutscher Verlag, 1996), pp. 157–171.

29. Eugen Kogon, Hermann Langbein, and Adalbert Rückerl, *Les Chambres à gaz, secret d'Etat* (Paris: Seuil, 1986).

6

THE GERMANS AND THE GENOCIDE

EVER SINCE THE 1980s, investigations into the attitude of Europeans at the time of the extermination of the Jews have been steadily gaining in width and depth. At first the attention of the public and the works of historians concentrated on those directly responsible: the Nazis who made the decisions and those who implemented them. Then it was time to examine the behavior of the states and peoples of the occupied countries, such as the Vichy regime and the French population. Next came the turn of the Allies, first and foremost the British and the Americans, who were criticized for their tardiness in offering a welcome to Jewish refugees before the war and for their procrastination in denouncing the genocide even as the drama was proceeding. Finally, it was those who remained neutral who found themselves in the dock, Switzerland in particular, by reason of the close economic ties that it maintained with Nazi Germany and the way that it closed its frontiers to those fleeing persecution. It came to be felt that everyone had played some role or other and so bore a measure of responsibility for the genocide, and that passivity, even when disapproving, had facilitated the task of the Nazis. Nowadays executioners, accomplices, and witnesses are all, indissociably, regarded as actors in the tragedy.[1]

All the same, the attitude of the Germans, the German population as a whole, still remains a subject of particular interest, as the response to Daniel Goldhagen's *Hitler's Willing Executioners* has clearly shown.[2] Goldhagen paints an exceptionally forceful picture of the violence of the Nazi killers, concentrating not on the best-known aspect of the genocide, namely the industrial gassing and suffocation of 3 million Jews, but rather its blood-drenched aspect, which brought death by the bullet to over 1.5 million Jews in Poland and the USSR, and killed at least tens of thousands of others, who died as a result of the brutality meted out in labor camps or on "death marches" on the eve of liberation. On those death marches, as many as tens of thousands of killers found themselves face to face with their victims—men, women and children, whose heads they split open and whose bodies they lashed without respite.

Goldhagen weaves into his study of this blood-soaked aspect of the genocide a twofold thesis that has elicited a barrage of criticisms from historians.[3] First, he maintains that these killers were motivated by a fierce zeal that could only have stemmed from deeply rooted anti-Semitism. He rejects the whole spectrum of motivations suggested by the historian Christopher Browning,[4] in whose view anti-Semitism was a necessary but not a sufficient condition for mass murder. According to him, other factors such as group pressure and the war context also played a part in turning "ordinary men" into pitiless executioners. When Goldhagen insists, on the contrary, that there was something that predestined the

Germans to murder the Jews, he takes little account of the context that liberated those men from the inhibitions of ordinary life and from the hold over them previously exerted by the normal institutional framework, a context that could encourage them to turn to mass crimes.

Moreover, by concentrating on the German killers and attributing to their behavior one single source—namely, the German national culture—he leaves in the shadows the role played by countless auxiliaries, ranging from those who participated in the pogroms of Romania to the Baltic and Ukrainian henchmen employed by the Nazis to execute their victims or to guard the camps. Besides, when he singles out the persecution of the Jews from the wider spectrum of Nazi violence, he overlooks the fact that those same German soldiers and policemen liquidated countless non-Jewish civilians in eastern Europe with no less ferocity. In Byelorussia, for example, they shot not only between 500,000 and 550,000 Jews, but also almost as many non-Jews—men, women, and children—some on suspicion of aiding the partisans, others for purely political or racial reasons.[5]

Goldhagen's second thesis is that those killers acted with the support of their compatriots. He claims that, given the opportunity, any German would have done as they did. His explanation for that hypothetical support is the presence of a virulent anti-Semitism that, as early as the nineteenth century, exalted the elimination of the Jews to the level of a "national project." This thesis too has attracted criticism from a number of specialists. It is reminiscent of the analysis that Emile Durkheim produced during World War I, in which he suggested that the violations of the rights of warfare com-

mitted by the soldiers of the German imperial army were
the product of a "national mentality" that had, so to speak,
programmed their behavior.[6] Durkheim, though, at least refrained from asserting, as Goldhagen somewhat inconse-
quentially did, that the soldiers thus programmed were
furthermore "willing" killers.

It certainly was the German people that produced these
pitiless brutes. But were the Germans as a whole a people of
pitiless brutes? The reply from specialists is far more quali-
fied, albeit not very precise. The documentation relating to a
study of German public opinion under Nazism (consisting
of recorded reports by the police, a host of party and state
organs, or in personal diaries) is abundant, but the persecution of the Jews is seldom mentioned, least of all during the
war years.[7] It is therefore hard to produce any more than a
reconstruction of tendencies, for we are obliged to do without any detailed knowledge of the opinions that prevailed in
particular regions, confessions, and social circles.

First, however, we should bear in mind that even before
the outbreak of war, German society was steeped in anti-
Semitism.[8] The distrust of Jews nurtured by Christianity
merged with the prejudice propagated by modern anti-
Semitism, and into this the regime dripped the poison of its
racist ideology, which exerted a particularly strong influence
upon the younger generations. A small minority of Germans
from the liberal bourgeoisie or Catholic and left-wing circles
deplored the fate of the Jews. Another minority, more substantial and above all more active, consisted of convinced
anti-Semites, who were particularly numerous among the
Hitlerjugend and the SA. These lost no opportunity to ex-

press their hatred with physical force and to call for further measures of persecution. Meantime, most Germans avoided taking sides and kept their distance. However, all the indications suggest that these people did accept the regime's policy of discrimination, exclusion, and emigration, particularly when it was dressed up in forms of legality. Hence the favorable reception they accorded to the Nuremberg laws and, conversely, their disapproval at the time of *Kristallnacht*—disapproval above all of the violence and disorder by which it was marked.

After the outbreak of war, the same tendencies persisted, but with two modifications. On the one hand, there was a hardening in the attitude of activists, and on the other, a growing indifference on the part of most Germans. The hardening attitude of the activists went hand in hand with the growing violence of the regime's anti-Semitic policies, and enabled the latter to recruit all the torturers and executioners that it needed. A similar hardening of attitudes affected the militant members of the Nazi party in the Reich, for the war situation, particularly the Allied bombing raids, furnished further motivation for their hatred of the Jews.

Meanwhile, as the organs of the regime noted with dissatisfaction, the indifference of most Germans was becoming more marked, despite the fact that propaganda drawing attention to the menace represented by the Jews was all the time intensifying. Yet the greater bulk of the population remained unreceptive, or at any rate refrained from taking up any definite position, except on a few exceptional occasions. One of these was in the autumn of 1941, when the wearing of a yellow star became obligatory for Jews and Jews began

to be deported. At this point, as in November 1938, alongside signs of approval, disagreement and compassion were
expressed, although they did not amount to a movement of
opposition based on principle, so they soon died away.

That indifference is bemusing for two reasons. In the first
place, it coincided with a period when the persecution was
entering its most murderous phase, and this could not possibly have been kept totally secret. Snippets of information
and, above all, many rumors were circulating more or less
everywhere. Many soldiers on the eastern front had witnessed the firing squads dispatching Jews, and by the summer of 1941 news of this had made its way back to Germany.
Then, above all from 1943 on, there were rumors—admittedly vague and distorted—about the gassing operations,
many of them based on reports broadcast by the Allied radio
services. Clearly, not many ordinary Germans were in a position to form a comprehensive overall view of the genocide.
On the other hand, many certainly were able to come by sufficient scraps of information to understand that the Jews
were the subjects of an unprecedented tragedy at the hands
of a regime whose toughness was affecting all and sundry.
The appalling life of concentration-camp detainees, who had
become extremely visible as they worked in their thousands
in external commandos as well as the reprehensible treatment of the foreign workers dispersed throughout the Reich
and the pitiless repression of resistance movements in occupied countries were common knowledge out in the public
domain.

Second, it is certainly not the case that the above-mentioned indifference signified that anti-Semitic prejudice was receding or on the wane. During the war period, xenophobia and popular racism peaked, stimulated by the massive presence of foreigners: by 1944, over seven million prisoners of war and forced laborers were working in appalling conditions in the Reich. Moreover, anti-Semitism continued to orient the views of most Germans. That is documented by many sources of evidence, ranging from requests from religious congregations demanding that converted Jews be excluded from their church services, through proposals formulated by the conservative resistance, which favored the introduction of a Jewish statute in postwar Germany,[9] to the high degree of anti-Semitism evident among German prisoners of war in the hands of the Allies.

What can be the explanation for this paradoxical situation of an anti-Semitic people that paid scarcely any attention to the fate of the Jews, even when these were being flung into the depths of the abyss? Two possible interpretations present themselves. According to one, the Germans were indifferent because the Jews occupied no more than a marginal place on the horizon of their lives,[10] for by now, within the Reich, the Jews had been reduced to a very small group. They were concentrated in the larger towns (half of them being resident in Berlin), where the regime had turned them into pariahs even before beginning to deport them. And meanwhile the Germans had trials and tribulations of their own to cope with that blunted their attention to others and closed their ears to the rumors of atrocities. Isolated and depersonalized as they were, the Jews, despite all the official propaganda, no longer attracted the attention of a people who were themselves confronted with life-threatening challenges.

The other interpretation detects conflicting attitudes beneath the surface indifference.[11] The choice that Germans made to distance themselves from the situation is analyzed as a move that enabled individuals to avoid any personal implication in this tragedy; although they did perceive its gravity, at the same time it placed them, personally, in an uncomfortable position. The fact that the gravity was indeed perceived is borne out by the widespread belief that the Allied bombing raids represented reprisals for the brutalities inflicted on the Jews. However, that perception made for an uncomfortable position since, unlike the Nazi Party, which was now largely discredited, Hitler himself still remained popular. He was the very personification of Germany, as was testified by the popular reaction to the news of his attempted assassination in July 1944. Germans distanced themselves from the extermination policy, which shocked them and made them fear for the future of their country, but to manifest disapproval or, worse still, to condemn it would have implied a tension or rupture vis-à-vis the regime, to which they remained linked and whose anti-Semitic policies they had accepted right from the start. This might also explain their attitude later on: after the war, Germans continued to repress all that they had already been repressing during it.

It is hard to choose between those two interpretations with any certainty. Besides, they seem not so much antagonistic as complementary. Whether the fate of the Jews was a matter of marginal importance on the far horizon of the

Germans' perceptions or whether it was they themselves, consciously or unconsciously, who marginalized it makes no difference to the reality of their passivity and the moral indifference upon which it rested. That passivity is all the more striking given that, at the very same time, German public opinion did indicate signs of its unequivocal disagreement with the regime's leaders. When the mentally sick were being exterminated, growing popular distress and the condemnatory position adopted by high-ranking members of the Catholic clergy did eventually alarm Hitler, who thereupon decided to suspend the operation. Would he have been equally flexible if his fellow citizens—individuals and the Churches alike—had manifested similar emotions in favor of the Jews? It seems unlikely. But the fact is that Hitler was never forced to face that question, and the German Jews were sent off to Auschwitz, abandoned by even the thoughts of their compatriots.

NOTES

1. See Raul Hilberg, *Perpetrators, Victims, Bystanders: The Jewish Catastrophe, 1933–1945* (Cambridge: Polity Press, 1996).

2. Daniel Goldhagen, *Hitler's Willing Executioners: Ordinary Germans and the Holocaust* (London: Little Brown, 1996).

3. On reception in Germany, see Julius H. Schoeps, ed., *Ein Volk von Mördern? Die Dokumentation zur Goldhagen-Kontroverse um die Rolle der Deutschen im Holocaust* (Hamburg: Verlag Hoffmann und Campe, 1996).

In France, see the documentation in *Le Débat* (January–February 1997), *L'Histoire* (January 1997), *Documents,* and *Les Temps modernes* (February–March 1997), and the essay by Edouard Husson, *Une culpabilité ordinaire? Hitler, les Allemands et la Shoah* (Paris: François-Xavier de Guibert, 1997).

4. Christopher Browning, *Ordinary Men: Reserve Police Batallion 101 and the Final Solution in Poland* (New York: HarperCollins, 1992).

5. Christian Gerlach, *Kalkulierte Morde. Die deutsche Wirtschaftsund Vernichtungspolitik in Weissrussland 1941 bis 1944* (Hamburg: Hamburger Edition, 1999), p. 1158.

6. Emile Durkheim, *"L'Allemagne au-dessus de tout": la mentalité allemande et la guerre* (Paris: Colin, 1915 [reprinted 1991]).

7. See Marlise Steinert, *Hitlers Krieg und die Deutschen. Stimmung und Haltung der deutschen Bevölkerung im Zweiten Weltkrieg* (Dusseldorf: Econ Verlag, 1970).

8. See Saul Friedländer, *L'Allemagne nazie et les Juifs. 1. Les Années de persécution (1933–1939)* (Paris: Seuil, 1997).

9. Christoph Dipper, "Der Widerstand und die Juden," in Jürgen Schmädeke and Peter Steinbach, eds., *Der Widerstand gegen den Nationalsozialismus* (Munich: Piper), pp. 598–616.

10. This interpretation has been defended in particular by Ian Kershaw, in *Popular Opinion and Political Dissent in the Third Reich: Bavaria, 1933–1945* (Oxford: Clarendon Press, 1983), chs. 6 and 9. He partially reconsid-

ered his position in "German Popular Opinion and the 'Jewish Question,' 1939–1943: Some Further Reflections," in Arnold Pauker, ed., *Die Juden im national-sozialistischen Deutschland, 1933–1943* (Tübingen: J.C.B. Mohr, 1986), pp. 365–385.

11. See David Bankier, *The Germans and the Final Solution: Public Opinion under Nazism* (Oxford: Blackwell, 1992).

BIBLIOGRAPHY

INTRODUCTION

Aly, Götz. *"Endlösung." Völkerverschiebung und der Mord an den europäischen Juden.* Frankfurt-on-Main: Fischer, 1995.

Aly, Götz, and Susanne Heim. *Vordenker der Vernichtung. Auschwitz und die deutschen Pläne für eine neue europäische Ordnung.* Hamburg: Hoffmann and Campe, 1991.

Bartov, Omer. *Germany's War and Holocaust: Disputed Histories.* Ithaca: Cornell University Press, 2003.

Bauman, Zygmunt. *Modernity and the Holocaust.* Cambridge: Polity Press, (1989), 1991.

Durkheim, Emile. *La Mentalité allemande et la guerre.* Paris: Armand Colin, (1915), 1991.

Friedländer, Saul. *L'Allemagne nazie et les Juifs. 1. Les Années de persécution, 1933–1939.* Paris: Seuil, 1997.

Goldhagen, Daniel. *Hitler's Willing Executioners: Ordinary Germans and the Holocaust.* London: Little Brown, 1996.

Voegelin, Eric. *Les Religions politiques.* Paris: Cerf, 1994.

I. RESENTMENT AND APOCALYPSE

1. WHY GERMANY?

Berding, Helmut. *Histoire de l'antisémitisme en Allemagne.* Paris: Ed. de la Maison des sciences de l'homme, 1991.

Birnbaum, Pierre. *Un mythe politique: la "République juive".* Paris: Fayard, 1988.

Blaschke, Olaf. *Katholizismus und Antisemitismus im Deutschen Kaiserreich.* Göttingen: Vandenhoeck and Ruprecht, 1999.

Elias, Norbert. *The Germans: Power Struggles, the Development of Habitus in the Nineteenth and Twentieth Centuries.* London: Secker and Warburg, (1992), 1995.

Holz, Klaus. *Nationaler Antisemitismus. Wissenssoziologie einer Weltanschauung.* Hamburg: Hamburger Edition, 2001.

Katz, Jacob. *Hors du ghetto. L'émancipation des juifs en Europe, 1770–1870.* Paris: Hachette, 1984.

Korinman, Michel. *Deutschland über alles: le pangermanisme, 1890–1945.* Paris: Fayard, 1999.

Langmuir, Kevin. *Toward a Definition of Anti-Semitism.* Berkeley: University of California Press, 1990.

Poliakov, Léon. *Histoire de l'antisémitisme.* Paris: Seuil, 1991, 2 vol.

Pulzer, Peter. *Jews and the German State: The Political History of a Minority, 1848–1933.* Oxford: Blackwell, 1992.

————. *German Anti-Semitism Revisited*. Rome: Archivio G. Izzi, 1999.

Puschner, Uwe. *Die völkische Bewegung im wilhelminischen Kaiserreich*. Darmstadt: Wissenschaftliche Buchgesellschaft, 2001.

Rohrbacher, Stefan, and Michael Schmidt. *Judenbilder. Kulturgeschichte antijüdischer Mythen und antisemitescher Vorurteile*. Hamburg: Rowohlt, 1991.

Volkov, Shulamit. *Antisemitismus als kultureller Code*. Munich: Beck, 2000.

Winock, Michel. *Nationalisme, Antisémitisme et Fascisme en France*. Paris: Seuil, 1982, 1990.

2. JUDEOPHOBIA AND THE NAZI IDENTITY

Ayçoberry, Pierre. *The Social History of the Third Reich, 1933–1945*. New York: The New Press, 1999.

Bärsch, Claus-Ekkehard. *Die politische Religion des Nationalsozialismus*. Munich: Fink Verlag, 2002.

Burleigh, Michael, and Wolfgang Wipperman. *The Racial State: Germany, 1933–1945*. Cambridge: Cambridge University Press, 1991.

Frei, Norbert. *L'Etat hitlérien et la société allemande, 1933–1945*. Paris: Seuil, 1994.

Jäckel, Eberhard. *Hitler idéologue*. Paris: Calmann-Lévy, 1973.

Kershaw, Ian. *Hitler, 1889–1936*. London: Allen Lane, 1998; *Hitler, 1936–1945*. London: Allen Lane, 2000.

Kroll, Frank-Lothar. *Utopie als Ideologie. Geschichtsdenken und politisches Handeln im Dritten Reich.* Paderborn: Schöningh, 1999.

Mommsen, Hans. *Auschwitz, 17 Juli 1942. Der Weg zur europäischen "Endlösung der Judenfrage."* Munich: DTV, 2002.

Peukert, Detlev, ed. *Die Reihen fast geschlossen: Beiträge zur Geschichte des Alltags unterm Nationalsozialismus.* Wuppertal: Hammer, 1981.

3. RESENTMENT AND APOCALYPSE

Bankier, David. *The Germans and the Final Solution: Public Opinion under Nazism.* Oxford: Blackwell, 1992.

Bankier, David, ed. *Probing the Depths of German Anti-Semitism: German Society and the Persecution of the German Jews. 1933–1941.* New York: Berghahn Books, 2000.

Bartov, Omer. *Hitler's Army: Soldiers, Nazis, and the War in the Third Reich.* Oxford: Oxford University Press, 1991.

Browning, Christopher. *Ordinary Men: Reserve Police Batallion 101 and the Final Solution in Poland.* New York: HarperCollins, 1992.

———. *Nazi Policy, Jewish Workers, German Killers.* Cambridge: Cambridge University Press, 2000.

Gerlach, Christian. *Krieg, Ernährung, Völkermord: Forschungen zur deutschen Vernivhtungspolitik im Zweiten Weltkrieg.* Hamburg: Hamburger Edition, 1998.

Longerich, Peter. *Politik der Vernichtung. Eine Gesamt-darstellung der nationalsozialistischen Judenverfolgung in Ostgalizien, 1941–1944.* Munich: Piper, 1998.

Pohl, Dieter. *Nationalsozialistische Judenverfolgung in Ostgalizien, 1941–1944.* Munich: Oldenbourg, 1997.

Roseman, Mark. *Ordre du jour: génocide. La conférence de Wannsee et la Solution finale.* Paris: Audiberti, 2002.

Solchany, Jean. "La violence nazi," *Revue d'histoire moderne et contemporaine,* April–June 2000.

Voegelin, Eric. *Hitler et les allemands.* Paris: Seuil, 2003.

II. FASCISM, NAZISM, AUTHORITARIANISM

The essays published in this collection are versions, revised and brought up to date, of texts that originally appeared with the following titles and in the following periodicals:

4. THE SPECTRUM OF ACCEPTANCE

"Régime nazi et société allemande," in Henry Rousso, ed., *Stalinisme et Nazisme, Histoire et mémoire comparées.* Brussels: Complexe, 1999, pp. 129–144.

5. A CONGENITAL VIOLENCE

"La violence congénitale du nazisme," in Henry Rousso, ed., *Stalinisme et Nazisme, Histoire et mémoire comparées.* Brussels: Complexe, 1999, pp. 129–144.

6. THE GERMANS AND THE GENOCIDE

"Les Allemands, un peuple de bourreaux?" *Les Collections de l'Histoire,* no. 3, October 1998, pp. 44–48.